Rejoice!
The King is Lord

Cover to Cover Bible Discovery

PHILIPPIANS

Rejoice!
The King is Lord

PHILIP GREENSLADE

Contents

Preface

Welcome to the first Christian church in Europe, meeting in the Macedonian city of Philippi, and to Paul's letter to it.

Philippians is a short letter and so full of warm, personal spiritual nourishment, that it incites us to love God more. This should not be read as implying that Philippians is 'gospel-lite'; far from it, it packs a powerful theological punch and sharply challenges us to live out what Gordon Fee calls the 'cruciform lifestyle'.[1]

Philippians is often treated as if it were all sweetness and light, a kind of first-century greetings card, untouched by the harsh realities of politics and economics. Nothing could be further from the truth. It is addressed to a brave and resilient group of believers called to live out the cross-shaped life in a society dominated by rigid Imperial ways of handling money, status and power. In such an atmosphere, Christians could only be regarded as subversives following a revolutionary Lord whose lifelong self-giving unto death had resulted in His elevation to the highest name and very throne of God. Local Imperial authority would be baffled by this allegiance to a superior kingdom; Caesar would be upstaged; Rome would be rattled.

So let it be today.

The title of this small book, borrowed from Tom Wright, is a playful twist on a much-loved hymn by Charles Wesley. It seeks to make an important biblical point. As Psalm 2 shows, God always intended that His king in Israel should one day become Lord of the world. In Jesus God has achieved His aim, and we can rejoice that Israel's true King (Messiah) is the world's rightful Lord.

I want to thank all those enthusiastic Bible Discovery 'Weekenders' at Waverley Abbey House whose hunger for God's Word has so encouraged my ministry. I appreciate, too, the members of Ewhurst Evangelical Church with whom these reflections were also shared.

My thanks are again due to the superb editorial and design team at CWR, and to my wife, Mary for her loving support.

I pray that our time spent with Paul's lovely letter will prove a disturbing and comforting experience!

Above all I hope it will refocus our hearts and minds on the Lord Jesus, the source of all our joy.

Philip Greenslade
2003

Seven things worth knowing about the Philippian letter

Philippians was written to Christians living in an Imperial outpost

If we pay attention to the setting of the letter we will be in a better position to feel the force of what Paul says.

Philippi was a military colony of Rome. The city had been refounded by the Emperor Octavian after military victory in 42 BC, renamed in honour of his daughter Philippi and repopulated with freedmen and veterans from the Roman Army.

Nowhere outside Italy was there any city more thoroughly Roman. It had been granted the high honour of the '*ius Italicum*', that is, of being governed by Roman law. In Ben Witherington's words, 'The Philippians would have a very good idea what it meant to live by ruling principles that originated from afar.'[2]

Paul urges his readers to live out their 'citizenship in heaven' (3:20), memorably paraphrased by James Moffatt as '*you are a colony of heaven*'. This is not an exact translation, but vividly captures the political flavour of Paul's language.

No one could have been in a better position to appreciate what it meant to live as a 'resident alien' than a believer who lived both 'in Philippi' and 'in Christ' (1:1) as a citizen of heaven in a colony of Rome.

Furthermore, even as Paul wrote, the Roman emperors were beginning to annex to themselves the titles Lord and Saviour. Nowhere outside of Rome would this have been taken more seriously than in the Roman colony of Philippi. Nowhere would the challenge to acknowledge another Lord and Saviour – Jesus – have been felt more keenly than by the Christians in Philippi (2:11; 3:20).

Richard Horsley has urged that we take more seriously the heavily political nuance in the Pauline notion of church as 'assembly'. The roots are indeed in the Greek Old Testament's description of Israel as the 'assembly' (or *ecclēsia*) of the Lord. But this, in Horsley's view, is conjoined with what was its normal connotation in the Greek-speaking Eastern Roman Empire – the citizen assembly which formed the key element in the local government of the Greek *polis*. Christian *ecclēsiai* then, must be viewed as the counterpart to these local political assemblies, the gathering by contrast of those whose 'citizenship' (*politeuma*) was in heaven (Phil. 1:27; 3:20), worshipping together as alternative communities, owning a higher allegiance than to the Emperor, the sign, foretaste and agent of a superior kingdom.[3]

For the Early Church in first-century Philippi, therefore, to confess Jesus as 'Lord' (Phil. 2:5–11) and to await Him as 'Saviour' (Phil. 3:20–21) was to commit a political and counter-cultural act. To do this was to relativise the Emperor and the Empire that went with him.[4]

'Rejoice the King is Lord' represents an outrageous re-alignment of political realities: Jesus, not Caesar, is Lord.

To await this one Lord's 'presence' or 'arrival', His *parousia* (a word regularly used for an Imperial visit),[5] was to look beyond what Rome offered for ultimate peace and security.

Philippians was written to Christians who were not wealthy or powerful

At the time of Paul's writing, it is estimated that the population of Philippi was about 15,000 inhabitants. The populace was probably two-thirds Greek and one-third Roman, the Romans being the descendants of the original veteran colonists and of basically Italian stock. These were augmented by freed slaves. The more numerous Greeks were either native or immigrants – only a few of whom would have been granted Roman citizenship.

In other words, Greeks were in a majority, but the Romans were in power. This is reflected in the fact that virtually all the inscriptions excavated at the site have been in Latin.

Latest estimates of the social categories of the populace suggest only 1 per cent elite landowners, 15 per cent colonist farmers, with nearly 40 per cent classified as slaves or poor. The largest group, it is thought, were *craftworkers and small traders*, like Lydia who was an immigrant from Asia dealing in purple cloth (Acts 16:14), and much like Paul, himself, who made his living by tentmaking. It was among these service providers that Paul tended to socialise and evangelise. This group was by no means wealthy and were economically vulnerable. Other occupations attested by inscription included town-crier, cashier, actors and stage manager and doctor.

This social mix was probably reflected in the church. However, most were craftworkers or service providers like Lydia, and most were Greeks, few of whom were actual Roman colonists – though some like the jailer presumably were.

But the church began with probably fewer than two dozen people: Lydia, with two or three Asian relatives and perhaps half-a-dozen slaves; the slave girl who had been delivered from demons, and the jailer, together with his family. So, perhaps, three Roman adults, plus three children and seven or more Asians formed the nucleus of this, the first ever church in Europe!

Philippians was written to Christians who were beginning to suffer economic hardship for their faith and witness to Christ

The Philippians were, it seems, a suffering church (1:29). In this they mirrored Paul's own mistreatment at the hands of the Roman Imperial authorities. What was the nature of their suffering? Certainly the church was being troubled by false teachers, as 3:3ff. shows, but the main opposition, it seems, was external to the church (1:28).

Recent research argues persuasively that their suffering was predominantly *economic*. The land-based economy of Philippi meant that almost everyone – from service providers down to the very poorest people – were dependent on Roman money.[6]

Everyday life was, to an unusual degree, governed by Roman authority, laws and habits. For example, take the case of a Christian baker supplying bread to commuting farmers and the local elite. Post conversion, our Christian baker might lose customers, and more crucially the use of his fellow baker's ovens for an unexpected larger order of bread. He might stop paying his subscription to the bakers' burial club, while his wife might remove the shrine of the local god from their shop. Suspect now through being part of a secretive association, the baker might arouse suspicion of troublemaking and be hauled before the magistrates and perhaps receive a beating.

This snapshot of life in first-century Philippi, is indebted to the recent research of Peter Oakes. In his words, 'the crucial form of suffering was economic. Broken relationships, broken reputations, and broken heads would all be serious forms of suffering in themselves. However for a family on subsistence income, the most serious aspects of each of these would be the long-term economic effect that it produced'.[7]

Writing to the Corinthians about the progress of his collection for the poor, which was so dear to his heart, Paul evokes the example of the Macedonian believers. 'Out of the most severe trial, their overflowing joy and their *extreme poverty* welled up in rich generosity' (2 Cor. 8:2, my italics).

Philippians was written to Christians who needed each other as a life-support system

The economic pressures being felt by the believers in Philippi would account for the apostle's urgent plea for unity in the church (1:27). Fellowship for them was not some ethereal, spiritual bonding, but a practical down-to-earth support system. In this unity, no one was out for his own interests but was concerned for the interests of others (2:1–4).

> In order to survive the breakdown of those relationships on which economic viability depended, 'what the Christians would need to do is to enter into a new set of economic and other relationships among themselves'.[8]

Relatively 'better-off' believers risked much to help their fellow members of the Body of Christ. They risked losing wealth, perhaps having to sell land; they risked losing valuable relationships with their pagan neighbours and being viewed as dishonourable; they risked being seen to provoke disorder and thus arouse the hostility of the local magistrates.

The reassurance that God would 'supply their need' was therefore *not* a recipe for a self-serving 'prosperity' gospel but a stark necessity for brave and cheerful subsistence-level earners learning to rely on grace in all circumstances.

In this giving and receiving, everyone could rely upon the confidence that God was well able to meet their need, out of His riches in Christ Jesus.

Philippians was written to persuade them that joy was possible in all circumstances

If the New Testament, as has been said, is 'the most joyful book in the world', Philippians has been rightly called '*the Letter of Joy*'. Joy as a theme is everywhere present in it and the atmosphere of joy pervasive.

Philippians is a much visited site not least because it shows us Paul at his warmest and most personal. This joy surges up even through trials and suffering (1:12–16). At its heart is a memorable celebration of Jesus in His self-giving, sacrifice and vindication. '*Rejoice the King is Lord!*' And again I say rejoice! From among the different types of letter current in the ancient world, Gordon Fee characterises Philippians as a 'letter of friendship'. It was a friendship forged in the fires of love and joy.

Philippians was written to thank them for gifts received

Philippians, written around AD 62, must be the most famous '*thank-you' note* in history!

Paul wrote to warn against false teachers and disunity but also to thank the Philippians for their continued sponsorship of his ministry. He thanks them for their long-term support for the gospel and his apostolic mission. He thanks them for their current support for him in prayer and giving during his imprisonment. He elsewhere acknowledges their generosity in contributing beyond their means to the collection for the needy church in Jerusalem (2 Cor. 8:1–3). Now he appreciates their monetary gift sent in the safe keeping of Epaphroditus who has stayed on as his personal assistant to console and care for him while in prison (1:5; 2:25; 4:14–19).

This mutual 'giving and receiving' in 'social reciprocity is the primary "stuff" of Graeco-Roman friendship'.[9]

Philippians was written to bolster their confidence in the triumph of the gospel and in the sovereignty of God over all other powers

Paul's affection for the Philippians is only eclipsed by his passion for the gospel which burns through the pages of this letter. The gospel is Paul's 'magnificent obsession' (1:5,7,12,15–17,27).

Paul celebrates the strange sovereignty, which works providentially to override Roman Imperial authority in order to manifest the kingdom of God and to exhibit the Lordship of Jesus Christ in every circumstance – whether imprisonment or economic hardship.

'Theology in Philippians', as Gordon Fee has well put it, 'first of all takes the form of a story'.[10] Central to the message of Philippians are the inter-related – though unequal – stories of Jesus (2:5–11) and Paul himself (3:4–14).

Paul also makes it crystal clear that Christian faithfulness is not an escapist trip out of difficulty or deprivation – as in some forms of so-called 'health and wealth gospels' – but is a victory won in the very midst of poverty and plenty, suffering and wellbeing, through the grace which makes us *content* in any situation and *adequate* for any challenge (1:12, 19–26; 4:10–13). To claim less is to undervalue what Christ has achieved, but to claim more than this is to get ahead of ourselves and to forget that our full and final salvation – including our new bodies – is a salvation we are still waiting for (1:6; 3:20–21)!

Above all, Jesus Christ is the beating heart of this letter, which, in Gordon Fee's summary, 'points us to Christ, both for now and forever. Christ is the gospel; Christ is Saviour and Lord; thus Christ is our life; Christ is our way of life; Christ is our future; Christ is our joy: "to live is Christ: to die is gain"; and all to the glory of our God and Father. Amen.'[11]

Bear these things constantly in mind as together we seek to hear the message of Philippians.

How it all began

Acts 16:7-40

[7]When they came to the border of Mysia, they tried to enter Bithynia, but the Spirit of Jesus would not allow them to. [8]So they passed by Mysia and went down to Troas. [9]During the night Paul had a vision of a man of Macedonia standing and begging him, 'Come over to Macedonia and help us.' [10]After Paul had seen the vision, we got ready at once to leave for Macedonia, concluding that God had called us to preach the gospel to them.

Lydia's Conversion in Philippi
[11]From Troas we put out to sea and sailed straight for Samothrace, and the next day on to Neapolis. [12]From there we travelled to Philippi, a Roman colony and the leading city of that district of Macedonia. And we stayed there several days.

[13]On the Sabbath we went outside the city gate to the river, where we expected to find a place of prayer. We sat down and began to speak to the women who had gathered there. [14]One of those listening was a woman named Lydia, a dealer in purple cloth from the city of Thyatira, who was a worshipper of God. The Lord opened her heart to respond to Paul's message. [15]When she and the members of her household were baptised, she invited us to her home. 'If you consider me a believer in the Lord,' she said, 'come and

stay at my house.' And she persuaded us.

Paul and Silas in Prison

[16]Once when we were going to the place of prayer, we were met by a slave girl who had a spirit by which she predicted the future. She earned a great deal of money for her owners by fortune-telling. [17]This girl followed Paul and the rest of us, shouting, 'These men are servants of the Most High God, who are telling you the way to be saved.' [18]She kept this up for many days. Finally Paul became so troubled that he turned round and said to the spirit, 'In the name of Jesus Christ I command you to come out of her!' At that moment the spirit left her.

[19]When the owners of the slave girl realised that their hope of making money was gone, they seized Paul and Silas and dragged them into the market-place to face the authorities. [20]They brought them before the magistrates and said, 'These men are Jews, and are throwing our city into an uproar [21]by advocating customs unlawful for us Romans to accept or practise.'

[22]The crowd joined in the attack against Paul and Silas, and the magistrates ordered them to be stripped and beaten. [23]After they had been severely flogged, they were thrown into prison, and the jailer was commanded to guard them carefully. [24]Upon receiving such orders, he put them in the inner cell and fastened their feet in the stocks.

[25]About midnight Paul and Silas were praying and singing hymns to God, and the other prisoners were listening to them. [26]Suddenly there was such a violent earthquake that the foundations of the prison were shaken. At once all the prison doors flew open, and everybody's chains came loose. [27]The jailer woke up, and when he saw the prison doors open, he drew his sword and was about to kill himself because he thought the prisoners had escaped. [28]But Paul shouted, 'Don't harm yourself! We are all here!'

[29]The jailer called for lights, rushed in and fell trembling before Paul and Silas. [30]He then brought them out and asked, 'Sirs, what must

I do to be saved?'

[31]They replied, 'Believe in the Lord Jesus, and you will be saved – you and your household.' [32]Then they spoke the word of the Lord to him and to all the others in his house. [33]At that hour of the night the jailer took them and washed their wounds; then immediately he and all his family were baptised. [34]The jailer brought them into his house and set a meal before them; he was filled with joy because he had come to believe in God – he and his whole family.

[35]When it was daylight, the magistrates sent their officers to the jailer with the order: 'Release those men.' [36]The jailer told Paul, 'The magistrates have ordered that you and Silas be released. Now you can leave. Go in peace.'

[37]But Paul said to the officers: 'They beat us publicly without a trial, even though we are Roman citizens, and threw us into prison. And now do they want to get rid of us quietly? No! Let them come themselves and escort us out.'

[38]The officers reported this to the magistrates, and when they heard that Paul and Silas were Roman citizens, they were alarmed. [39]They came to appease them and escorted them from the prison, requesting them to leave the city. [40]After Paul and Silas came out of the prison, they went to Lydia's house, where they met with the brothers and encouraged them. Then they left.

This is the story of the first Christian converts in Europe! To say this is to be deliberately anachronistic, of course, since Asia and Macedonia were, at the time, merely two provinces of the Roman Empire. But from our standpoint Philippi was the first Christian church in what we now call 'Europe'! Mind you, it took the Holy Spirit to get the gospel there. Paul's apostolic team tried to go everywhere else – Asia, Bithynia – but the Holy Spirit vetoed every attempt to avoid 'Europe'!

Here is the first mark of *the strange sovereignty* that shapes this story: the Spirit releases and frees us and urges us out and on; the world is our parish, the ends of the earth the horizons of the Great

Commission. Yet He can prevent just as well (vv.6–7).

His restraints are the safeguard of our freedom. Asia and Bithynia are for another time and perhaps for other people: right now, Paul, Silas, Timothy I want you over here!

It was the vision that decided it (16:9)! Paul had a vision of a 'man of Macedonia'. How did he know that, I wonder; by the face, or the language spoken? It's worth recalling that Macedonia had been the power-base for the conquest of the then-known world by the most famous Macedonian of them all – Alexander the Great. Had Paul ever seen this as a challenge to the gospel of the kingdom?

Be that as it may, the four missionaries, convinced by the vision, set out in pursuit of a dream (16:10). Did we say 'four'? Yes; it seems that Paul, Silas and Timothy have been joined by the *fourth man*.

Significantly, here is the very first place in Luke's exciting narrative where the 'third person plural' gives way to the 'first person plural' – what *'they'* did changes into what *'we'* did. In other words, at this point the narrator joins the team and joins the tour! This is the point where *three* missionaries become *four*.

This is the point where Luke himself – as he recalls from his personal diary of events – joins the party! – '… *we* got ready … concluding that God has called *us* … from Troas *we* put to sea …' (vv.10–11, my italics).

After the 125-mile sea trip – north-west – the group arrived at the port of Neapolis (modern Kavalla) and then travelled some 10 miles west to Philippi (vv.11–12).

Philippi, Luke reminds us, was a Roman colony. The settlers, as was often the case, included Roman veterans demobbed from the army. Philippi was given the unusual status of being a legal part of Italy; Philippi, says Ben Witherington, was as it were, 'Rome in microcosm'.

What Luke records is a major transition in the apostolic mission away from largely Jewish audiences to mixed ones, and to encounters with Graeco-Roman religion, philosophy and political authority.

In Philippi we meet *three characters in search of an author*.

These three characters are:

- a purple-dealing businesswoman
- a python-possessed prophetess
- a panic-stricken prison chief.

The common factor linking their stories is Christ's gift of *freedom*.

'Freedom' is a well-worn, even politically correct term: a useful 'buzz' word to rouse the masses. 'Freedom' is part of the so-called 'feel-good' factor, a flag everyone waves. Freedom is top of everyone's agenda and every party's manifesto – freedom to think, speak, teach, worship – defined, if it is defined at all, as *freedom of choice*.

Our modern consumer culture is a supermarket of choice. Forty years ago our local food store had 500 items – now they stock over 12,000! Do I really need 80 different brands of breakfast cereal? Psychologists confirm that much neurosis is being caused by 'option-overload', being burdened with too many choices for comfort.

Acts 16 is about people who are *free* and people who are in *bondage*; but what is intriguing is to ask: Which is which? Which characters in the story are enslaved and which are free?[12]

Consider *Lydia* – the purple-dealing businesswoman (16:13–15)! She was, in all probability, a reasonably successful woman with her own house and business, dealing profitably in textiles – especially the purple-dyed cloth that featured in the power-dressing of the rich and influential of her day.

Paul's team found her on the Sabbath at prayer; so, evidently, she was a Jewish convert. But the group she joined met outside the city-gate by the river at an open-air site reserved for worship. It was not a synagogue because for that you needed at least ten men!

The strange sovereignty that has brought them to Philippi now strikes again (v.14). Lydia is opened up to faith and to believers baptism for her and her household. She immediately offers hospitality to the apostolic team and so, no doubt, a house church is born – the first in all Europe.

Throughout Acts, Luke graphically shows the gospel breaking through all barriers. Before it social and religious walls come crashing down. Significantly, but perhaps not surprisingly, the first convert in Europe is a woman! Jesus does more for women – even successful fashion-conscious career women – than feminism ever will. He truly sets them free.

Notice, further, what happens to the *demonised slave-girl* (16:16–18). She was possessed by a snake-spirit. This probably indicates that, like the oracle at Delphi, she was inspired by Apollo, who was believed to be embodied at Delphi in a python. She spoke like a ventriloquist and offered clairvoyant judgments. The syndicate who sponsored her exploited this occult ability for considerable profit. For them she was, no doubt in more ways than one, 'a nice little number'. Her outburst probably denotes pluralistic ideas about deities.

Roused finally to annoyance, Paul casts out the evil spirit 'in the name of Jesus' (v.18) and she is set free!

Free at last … free at last … I'm free at last …

Cry freedom; cry Philippi!

But her sponsors are not amused. Luke tells it with wit. He uses the same Greek word for 'came out' of the evil spirit in verse 18 as in verse 19 for 'gone' – of their hope of profit! As the demon went out of the woman, their profit margins went out of the window!

The Philippian Chamber of Commerce is outraged. For then – as now – economics rules all. Just as the pork merchants went mad when Jesus cast demons into their pigs, just as the Ephesus branch of the International Guild of Silversmiths went crazy when their trade in false gods was ruined at Ephesus, so here freedom threatens the power elites.

Already Luke has set up a fascinating contrast: the relatively well-off and generous Lydia making her home available and offering hospitality on the one hand: on the other, the avaricious owners of the slave-girl frantic at the prospect of lost profits.

The latter are frantic enough to stir the mob to xenophobic, anti-Semitic hatred which pushes the legal authorities into instant and savage injustice (v.20a). But it was a back-handed compliment: '[They] are throwing our city into an uproar.' Of course, the gospel of Jesus does that.

For the gospel of the kingdom in the power of the Spirit challenges every entrenched vested interest that enslaves men and women and corrupts human community. Wherever there is social stereotyping, sexual discrimination, demonic possession, economic exploitation – wherever there are practices and attitudes that cripple and dehumanise – the *gospel of truth invades to bring life and liberation.*

Whether self-interested consumerism, nationalistic xeno-phobia, the cramping peer pressure of the crowds, the dead hand of traditional religion and customs – everything that binds and destroys – Jesus confronts with His offer of freedom. *Cry Jesus; cry freedom!*

This, too, was what the *prison-chief* discovered (16:25–40).

There is a jailer and there are prisoners, but who is free? 'Having the key to someone else's cell does not make you free'.[13]

Suddenly an earthquake shatters the calm – it's that strange sovereignty at work again: it shakes the building and the jailer. There's a shout for help: 'Get me out of this mess; rescue me.' But it's not the prisoners who are shouting it! They, bleeding, bruised and sleepless, are singing songs of freedom in the night!

It's the jailer who wants to be rescued!

It's the jailer who wants to get out of jail!

It's the prison governor who's desperate to be set free!

'*What do I have to do to get free?*' – it's not Paul or Silas but the jailer who asks this question; and it's the prisoners who have the answer! It's difficult to take the jailer's cry as anything other than a desperate plea to save his skin rather than his soul. He certainly wasn't inquiring about the four spiritual laws. But, like all of us when we first experience the grace of God, the jailer gets far more than he bargained for or deserved: 'Believe in the Lord Jesus, and you will be saved – you and your household' (16:31).

By the end of the story, the strange sovereignty that shapes this whole narrative empowers Paul to stand up for his rights as a Roman citizen (vv.35–40). Paul is emboldened with such great poise and composure that the authorities eventually apologise to him (v.39).

Asked to leave the city, the apostolic team do, but in their own time and at their own pace. In the strange sovereignty in which they move, they will not be hurried. So they take time to say goodbye to Lydia and the brothers and the baby-church before they take their leave.

By the end of the story, everyone who at first appeared to be free – the girl's owners, the judges, the jailer – is shown to be a slave! While everyone who at first appeared to be enslaved – the slave-girl, Paul and Silas – is free!

Cry freedom in Philippi.

The four missionaries have pursued their dream – at whatever cost – and the gospel of Jesus Christ is established in Europe.

The three characters in search of an author have found Him and He has re-written the script of their lives and set them free from acting any part but the truly human one of being in His drama. That is salvation. That is true freedom. And so in the joy of being rescued and liberated was born the first Christian church in what we now call Europe!

It was to this church that Paul wrote his letter to which we now turn.

Outline of the Letter to the Philippians

'Inextinguishable Blaze'

1:1–2	Greetings and introduction
1:3–6	Praise for the Philippians Partnership in the gospel
1:7–8	Passion for the gospel Affection for the Philippians
1:9–11	Prayer for the Philippians Perception in love

A Death-defying Leap of Faith

1:12–26 Irrepressible apostle – unstoppable gospel
Paul's imprisonment:
evangelises his enemies 1:12–13
encourages his friends 1:14
exploited by his rivals 1:15–18

Paul's aims and ambition
  exalting Christ in life or death 1:21–24
  expecting deliverance 1:25–26

1:27–2:4 Living lives worthy of the gospel
  standing together against opposition 1:27–30
  having a Christian mindset 2:1–4
  sharing together in humility 2:1–4

The Cruciform Mindset

2:5–11 The mindset of Jesus
  the historic story of Jesus
  the true story of Adam
  the fulfilled story of Israel
  the astonishing story of God!
  the revised story of the world.

Real Stars and True Celebrities

2:12–18 Working out your salvation
  spiritual work-out 2:12–13
  stars in His eyes 2:14–16
  sacrificial offering 2:17–18

2:19–30 Unsung heroes
  Timothy 2:19–24
  Epaphroditus 2:25–30

Revised Balance Sheet

3:1–4 True and false worship

3:4–16 Paul's story!
  failed confidence 3:4–6
  revised balance sheet 3:7–9
  knowing Jesus 3:10–11

PHILIPPIANS

1:1-2 Greetings and introduction

¹Paul and Timothy, servants of Christ Jesus,

To all the saints in Christ Jesus at Philippi, together with the overseers and deacons:

²Grace and peace to you from God our Father and the Lord Jesus Christ.

A friend and I agreed recently that it was unlikely we'd make it into *Who's Who*. We preferred, we said, to be in God's 'Who's Not'! – in the Lamb's Book of nobodies, made somebodies by grace and redemption. And this is not a Book of the Dead even for those who have died, but a Book of the Living for all who are His 'saints'.

The way Paul opens this letter shows us immediately what a remarkable change the gospel has brought about in human relationships. Usually leaders lord it over servants; usually 'saints' are the larger than life people who overawe the rank-and-file. But the gospel reverses this. Now the traffic flows in the opposite direction. Here the leaders are the servants writing to meet the needs of the saints!

It is Jesus who has made all the difference. In His light, social status is turned upside down. Measured by Him, we are all 'bondservants' – whether apostles, overseers, deacons or members of the church. Measured by what we are 'in Him', we are all 'saints' – apostles, people, even deacons!

Paul then does not celebrate saints set in stained-glass windows – though we thank God for them – but believers in Christ who give evidence of the gospel bound in shoe-leather, in the walking, talking, working lives of all 'saints in ordinary'. Christians are a rare breed, the only people able to live in two places at once, enjoying dual nationality *in* Christ, and *in* Philippi.

1:2

Conventional greetings in ancient letters began where we end, with the signature. But, as we know, Jesus transforms everything He touches, even letter openings! Here is a 'sanctified hello'.

The usual words are now enlarged and enriched with the rich language of the gospel. Our hellos are no mere empty phrases but sanctified greetings, imparting grace and bestowing peace.

So 'grace and peace to you' is a compressed message. This is not a greetings-card message of nice wishes but one with theological content which the letter will subsequently unpack.

As in his other correspondence, Paul invests the formal greetings with the full significance of what he intends to say and fill out in the rest of the letter. Already he has hinted at the servant-like humility that he will point to in Christ and urge the Philippians to emulate; already he has emphasised that all the Christians in Philippi are 'saints' and need therefore to agree with one another to maintain their unity. Now he foreshadows the substance of the message of grace and peace which he will go on to show is the basis of their fellowship in Christ, whether in suffering or service.

Isn't it amazing what can be conveyed in a 'hello'?

1:3–6 Praise for the Philippians: partnership in the gospel

[3]I thank my God every time I remember you. [4]In all my prayers for all of you, I always pray with joy [5]because of your partnership in the gospel from the first day until now, [6]being confident of this, that he who began a good work in you will carry it on to completion until the day of Christ Jesus.

Philippians must be the most famous 'thank you' note in history.

Paul wrote the letter to warn against false teachers and disunity but also to thank the Philippians for their continued sponsorship of his ministry. He thanks them for their long-term support for the gospel and his apostolic mission. He thanks them for their current support for him in prayer and giving during his imprisonment.

He elsewhere acknowledges their generosity in contributing beyond their means to the collection for the needy church in Jerusalem (2 Cor. 8:1–3). Now he appreciates their monetary gift sent in the safe keeping of Epaphroditus who has stayed on as his personal assistant to console and care for him while in prison.

But Paul not only thanks them he *thanks God for them*! And notice how he does it. Every time they come into his mind he offers thanks to God for them! What a great way to remember people.

Spurgeon once said that there must be 'think' at the bottom of 'thank'. He meant that there ought to be intelligent content to our praise. But we can broaden that to suggest that it would be beneficial to us and to the Church if our thoughts of people turned to prayerful thanksgiving for them. People look different when we pray for them and especially if we thank God for them.

Why not pray right now for those people most on your mind. And perhaps now is the time to determine afresh to write that letter, make that phone call or send that gift as your way of saying: 'Thank you.'

1:4 '... I always pray with joy ...'

As we have said, joy as a theme is everywhere present in this letter and the atmosphere of joy pervasive. But what is 'joy' and where does it come from? Some distinctions are called for.

Pleasure comes to us usually *from* things through our senses – a gorgeous sunset, fine wine, a Rembrandt painting.

Happiness comes to us chiefly *from* events through people – a daughter's wedding, the birth of a grandchild. But all this is vulnerable to disappointment and tragedy and loss.

Joy, on the other hand, is *God-given*, coming to us *from Christ through the Spirit, and cannot be taken from us.*

Joy is not a passing mood but a deep-seated disposition of wellbeing derived from even deeper convictions about the truth of the way things are. Such joy springs from an inner exhilaration over what God has done for us and in others.

Joy is the exuberant buoyancy of confidence in God.

Joy is the resilience of spirit that can look at the worst and still believe in God's future.

As the blind hymnwriter, George Matheson sang: 'O Joy that seekest me through pain, I cannot close my heart to thee; I trace the rainbow through the rain, and feel the promise is not vain: that morn shall tearless be.'

1:5 Gospel partners

Paul's joy here is a glow of contentment that results from seeing the gospel advance whatever the opposition.

'Joy is the serious business of heaven,' said C.S. Lewis, no doubt reflecting on the fact that the angels rejoice over one sinner who repents.

Paul rejoices in praying for the Philippians because of their 'partnership in the gospel from the first day until now'.

Again we strike gold in another of the key words in the letter used to describe the quality of New Testament Christian living. This is the word '*koinonia*' – often translated 'fellowship' or, as here, 'partnership'.

It needs to be said that 'fellowship' is not essentially a warm, fuzzy feeling generated by a social event or even by a time of worship. The descriptive word '*koinonia*' implies 'to share in' something, to 'hold something in common' – whether an experience or an activity.

In the Christian case, this is not a sharing together but a sharing together *in* something else – in our case in Christ and in the Holy Spirit.

'*Koinonia*' originally described those in business partnership and implies bonds of commitment and co-operation. This is Paul's emphasis here. He applauds the Philippians for their faithful participation with him in the cause of the gospel. They have taken out shares in the mission of the gospel. Have we? Nothing gives greater joy.

1:6 No unfinished business

Dr Martyn Lloyd-Jones who disliked the idea of favourite texts, confessed that if pressed to have one, this would be it!

The 'good work' which God began in the lives of the Philippian Christians might refer to their support for Paul and his ministry. But the mention of the 'day of Christ' makes it more likely that this refers to the saving work of grace begun in their lives when they responded in repentant faith to the preaching of the gospel.

Of course, the good work the Philippians are doing in backing Paul's mission is in itself evidence of this larger work of grace in their lives. And, praise God, what God begins He completes. You may feel you are in the middle of the slow movement right now but our God composes no 'unfinished symphonies'. What He starts, He continues.

God never grows weary in well-doing. He never downs tools. He does not repent of His sacrifices. His purposes for our lives cannot be thwarted. What a comfort this is. Jesus finished the foundation work on the cross. God is committed to completing the building which has been laid on so costly a foundation.

We are saved in three tenses – we have been saved, we are being saved, we will be saved. God's good work covers all three – from commencement through continuation to completion! What grace!

'All's well that *starts* well!'

There is – we might say – an inextinguishable blaze that God has set alight in the heart of every true believer. It is a cause of ceaseless joy and confidence to realise how wonderfully God has taken the initiative in our salvation.

He has begun 'a good work' in our lives which cannot be thwarted. Our human decisions alone would be too shaky a basis for such confidence. But the unshakeable resolution of God is a firm reason for hope.

Our ultimate salvation, says Alec Motyer, can no more be 'forfeited than the father can break off his pledged promise to glorify his Son in the day of Christ'.[14]

In John Bunyan's vision, when Christian saw water being poured on the fire against the wall in *Pilgrim's Progress*, he initially feared that the work of grace would be extinguished by the devil. But his wonder grew when he saw how the flames burned higher and hotter. He was shown 'the backside of the wall where he saw a man with a vessel of oil in his hand, of the which he did also continually cast, but secretly, into the fire'. 'This' it was explained to him, 'is Christ who continually, with the oil of his grace maintains the work already begun in the heart'.

And there is a day of completion, a deadline if we can call it that when it is so full of life! The day of Christ awaits us. For all those willing to submit continually to God's dealings, it will be not just a judgment day of quality control on our lives but a glorious day of completion and consummation; a wonderful coming-out parade of these to whom God has applied the finishing touches.

1:7–8

> [7]It is right for me to feel this way about all of you, since I have you in my heart; for whether I am in chains or defending and confirming the gospel, all of you share in God's grace with me. [8]God can testify how I long for all of you with the affection of Christ Jesus.

Here two notes are struck:

1) Paul's passion for the gospel
2) Paul's affection for the Philippians

1) *Paul's passion for the gospel*
This is a particular emphasis in these opening statements (1:5,7,12,27).

But notice carefully what the gospel is. It is not the offer of new birth or forgiveness or justification: these are the saving spin-offs of trusting in Jesus.

Strictly speaking, the gospel is the public announcement through preaching of what God has done to and through Jesus, as is confirmed by the synonymous term 'preaching Christ' (1:15).

The gospel is the proclamation of His death, resurrection, exaltation and the announcement of Him as Messiah of Israel and Lord of the world.

As such, 'gospel' involves both the content of what is confessed and the actual activity of proclaiming this as a powerful message that changes people and transforms the way we construe the world as it is.

The good news of what God has done through Jesus Christ is his overriding obsession. For the sake of the gospel, Paul will risk life and limb. For the sake of the gospel he is now imprisoned and facing possible death. But his feelings are not bound up with his own plight. Paul's passion for the gospel is matched only by his affection for the Philippians.

2) *Paul's affection for the Philippians*
His heart goes out to the Philippians whom he loves with the affection of Jesus. Paul is a wholehearted and warmhearted man.

A student of mine, who had previously had the stereotypical image of Paul as a cold and hard man, came on a Bible Discovery course with CWR. She wrote later, 'Since coming to Waverley, my opinions have taken such a dramatic change … and I am beginning to understand just how far short of really understanding Paul my previous opinion was. Far from disliking people he very clearly loves the Christians in Philippi … He is clearly devoted to the people at Philippi. I begin to have great affection for this man who gave his life for Jesus.'

Then, as now, Paul can inspire and give great affection. But again notice he doesn't put himself on any pedestal. What matters to him is that he and his Philippian friends are sharers together in the same grace of God. Today, it remains true: you are our partners, we're in this together, readers and writers.

1:9–11 Paul's prayer for the Philippians

⁹And this is my prayer: that your love may abound more and more in knowledge and depth of insight, ¹⁰so that you may be able to discern what is best and may be pure and blameless until the day of Christ, ¹¹filled with the fruit of righteousness that comes through Jesus Christ – to the glory and praise of God.

We come now to consider Paul's prayer for the Philippians. This is his characteristic way of starting his letters. Prayer for the churches is a major priority. But it's striking also to see *what* Paul prays for. In nearly every case it is not for success or evangelism or growth in numbers but that his Christian readers may *get to know God* better. So it is here.

He prays that they might have 'more love'. And what he prays for is love that abounds, is lavish and generous, that keeps time with the beating heart of Jesus.

In modern society, the language of love is devalued currency. 'Love is blind' we say. But Christian love is *not* blind. In fact, Paul prays for love which has content and meaning, for love that 'overflows in *knowledge*'. God wants His love in us to be an informed love, a wise love with a moral quality about it which knows how to love in truth.

Paul prays for a love which has 'discernment'. Christian love is not a sudden adrenaline rush. We must not do our theology or worship only with our hormones.

From the word Paul uses here we derive the word 'aesthetics' – our appreciation of what is beautiful and good. G.H. Morrison once said that you could tell a person who loves books or flowers by the way they handle them. So, he said, you can tell a person who loves people by the way she handles them. To love with discernment is to practise tact and sensitivity. Love is a connoisseur in the art of appreciating people.

1:9 Perception in love

Paul wants his readers' love to be substantial and meaningful not airy-fairy. This is another case where passing moods must deepen into long-lasting attitudes. He prays that they develop a wise love because it will enable them to 'approve what is excellent'. Again, love is far from being blind.

True Christ-centred love acts like a quality control device to test the quality of metal. All that glitters in our glamorous society is not gold! True Christ-inspired love will help to separate the gold from the dross.

His love opens your eyes to how to value everything else in life by showing things up for what they really are. It enables you to 'recognise the highest and the best' (J.B. Phillips).

Love is not a 'one-size-fits-all' but provides a sense of what really matters. Jesus criticised the Pharisees for majoring on minors, for missing the wood for the trees, for trumpeting the trivial over the vital. Martyrs, someone once said, have to know how to discriminate between the important and the trivial. They have to know what's worth dying for! And if love will tell us what's worth dying for, it will surely guide us in what's worth living for.

1:10–11 Love's labours are never lost!

Paul's prayer invites us to reflect on the kind of people which true Christian love produces. Paul prays for a wise and discerning love so that his readers may be sincere and without offence until the day of Christ.

'Sun-judged' is the picture word Paul uses here. On recent railway journeys in Britain I have noticed how filthy the carriage windows are when the sun shines through. (Obviously when the UK's national rail network was sold off into private ownership, the dirt was left in the public's possession.) The sun shows up all the dirt.

To be sincere means that others can see right through you! Love makes you sincere and transparent. J.E. Rattenbury once remarked that apostles – and, we might add, all Christian believers – were meant not merely to be looked at but seen through!

Some ancient sculptors used cracked stone for their work, covering up the blemishes with wax. But when the sun shone the wax melted and revealed the flaws. Some people are like sweets with a hard centre and a soft surround. Melt away the sentimental outside and you find a hard, self-centred individual.

So we need to pray that God's love will do its deep work in us. Eventually 'fruits of righteousness' grow on the vine of love. This is not a politically correct love which immorally tolerates anything. This love creates goodness that will stand the scrutiny of the day of Christ and bring praise and glory to God.

Prayer and Reflection

Thank You, Lord, for the grace that has come to me from
  You through other people.
So much blessing in my life has come this way.
I am so glad that You are working in my life.
What You have begun in me is a deep and lasting work of grace
  that sustains me even today and will preserve me to the end.
Teach me patience in the slow movements and strengthen my
  faith in turbulent times.
Rekindle in Your Church a confidence in the gospel.
Despite all the disappointments, renew our love for each other.
Keep alive in me the joy of my salvation.
Help me to grow in discerning what is of real value.
Keep me alert to appreciate whatever is excellent wherever
  I find it.
Help me to love well and to love wisely
In Jesus' name.
Amen.

- Consider the intensity of Paul's passion for the gospel, his feelings for the Philippians, and his joy in Jesus: how deeply do we share such intensity?

- Measure your typical prayers against Paul's. Note what his prayer-priorities are. In the light of Paul's praying, should we change the way we pray or what we pray for?

- How can we discern 'what is best'?

- Explore the implications of C.S. Lewis's statement that 'joy is the serious business of heaven'.

A DEATH-DEFYING LEAP OF FAITH

PHILIPPIANS

1:12-26 Irrepressible apostle – unstoppable gospel

[12]Now I want you to know, brothers, that what has happened to me has really served to advance the gospel. [13]As a result, it has become clear throughout the whole palace guard and to everyone else that I am in chains for Christ. [14]Because of my chains, most of the brothers in the Lord have been encouraged to speak the word of God more courageously and fearlessly.

[15]It is true that some preach Christ out of envy and rivalry, but others out of good will. [16]The latter do so in love, knowing that I am put here for the defence of the gospel. [17]The former preach Christ out of selfish ambition, not sincerely, supposing that they can stir up trouble for me while I am in chains. [18]But what does it matter? The important thing is that in every way, whether from false motives or true, Christ is preached. And because of this I rejoice.

Yes, and I will continue to rejoice, [19]for I know that through your prayers and the help given by the Spirit of Jesus Christ, what has happened to me will turn out for my deliverance. [20]I eagerly expect and hope that I will in no way be ashamed, but will have sufficient courage so that now as always Christ will be exalted in my body, whether by life or by death. [21]For to me, to live is Christ and to die is gain. [22]If I am to go on living in the body, this will mean fruitful labour for me. Yet what shall I choose? I do not know! [23]I am torn between the two: I desire to depart and be with Christ, which is better by far; [24]but it is more necessary for you that I remain in the body. [25]Convinced of this, I know that I will remain, and I will continue with all of you for your progress and joy in the faith, [26]so that through my being with you again your joy in Christ Jesus will overflow on account of me.

This remarkable passage again speaks volumes for the way the gospel transforms our view of reality.

Paul would argue that even prison looks different if you're there for the sake of the gospel. This is what matters most to Paul; not his own interests, or the danger of his own situation but the strange opportunities it presented for the furtherance of the gospel. He's not in prison for crime but for Christ.

This sovereignty, by which God's grace wrests good even out of evil circumstances, we call the providence of God.

'Providence' is a rather dull word for a sparkling truth. God's overarching strategy is very flexible in its tactics. God is infinitely adaptable and can work out His sovereign will in the most unfavourable conditions. This is Paul's deeply held conviction and it makes him remarkably resilient. Trying to tame him is like trying to take a tiger by the tail! What an irrepressible prisoner Paul is!

In 1637, that saintly Scotsman, Samuel Rutherford, like the apostle imprisoned for his faith, wrote from his cell: 'Christ triumphs in me. This is my palace not my prison. I think this is all, to gain Christ. All other things are shadows, dreams, fancies and nothing.'

Paul is spiritually buoyant. Suppressing this man is like trying to sink a cork in a bath! But Paul would only say, it's all Christ's doing and He can do the same for any believer in Him. The Holy Spirit can make you irrepressible whatever your circumstances. Whatever has happened to you, can you believe with Paul that it might somehow tend to the furtherance of the gospel?

1:13-18
Paul mentions three effects of his imprisonment.

1. Firstly, it *evangelises his enemies.* 'It has become clear thoughout the whole palace guard … that I am in chains for Christ.' No one is in any doubt why Paul is in prison: it is for Jesus. One member

of the Philippian church would have first listened to this letter read out, with a wry smile. In the local jail in Philippi he had once, as prison governor, locked up Paul and his companion, Silas, only to hear these two undaunted servants of Jesus fill the night air with songs of praise to God. Now, as a Christian himself, he understood the secret of being an 'ambassador for Jesus even in chains'.

2. If Paul's attitude to captivity effects his enemies, it *encourages his friends*. Far from being demoralised by his imprisonment, Paul says, they have been stimulated and emboldened to speak God's Word even more fearlessly than before (v.14).

3. Sadly, Paul admits, his situation is being *exploited by his rivals* whose envy and competitive spirit drove them to seek to take advantage of his absence to make a name for themselves. Amazingly even this doesn't faze Paul. In Galatians 1:8 he displays a very different attitude where the truth is at stake. Rival preachers he will tolerate, but rival gospels he will not.

It is worth noting what 'preaching Christ' entails. This is not a matter of inviting people to receive Him into their hearts. To 'preach Christ' is to make a public announcement that Christ not Caesar is Lord. This is what had got the apostle into trouble with the authorities and explains why he is writing from prison. 'Paul's rivals were no doubt copying his message precisely in order get him into more trouble'.[15]

1:19–20 These words are a veritable tapestry of grace

As we reflect on Paul's attitude to imprisonment, we can note how confidently he awaits his final salvation. Whatever happens to him meanwhile, whether captivity or release, death or life, is in God's hands and, he believes, can only work for his ultimate good.

One thinks here of Old Testament examples of this defiant attitude.

For instance, we might recall the story of Joseph told in Genesis 45:5–8; 50:19–20. Even more pertinent is the story of Job, especially Job 13:16, a text which is almost certainly echoed here in the very phrases Paul uses. (N.B. *'apobēstai eis sō tērian'* is a direct allusion to the Greek text of Job 13:16.) As if Paul sees his own experience of waiting for vindication mirroring Job's. It may even be that the rival preachers match Job's comforters in Paul's mind.

This is the poise that is possible to the Christ-centred life. After all when Paul was first imprisoned in Philippi the walls fell down; but this time – wherever Paul is imprisoned, whether Rome or Ephesus – there is no automatic escape route.

Paul believes this will turn out for his vindication so that he will 'not be put to shame' in the sense of being let down by God. Whether in the short term or in the longer eternal sense, deliverance will come. Like Job, he knows that his Redeemer lives and that he will stand in that day. But, as we have said, this is not automatic. He is sustained by the *prayers of others* and by his *own immediate experience of the Holy Spirit.*

God 'choreographs' the drama to supply the needed resources of the Spirit to Paul but whether He does it because others pray is the big question. God sovereignly interweaves our intercession and His intervention into the final tapestry of His strategic purpose. How He does this is the miracle and mystery of grace. But we can be assured that our prayers count for something in God's big scheme of things, usually in ways beyond our knowing. As long as we aim high at God's glory and the furtherance of the gospel, we remain free.

The British missionary, Geoffrey Bull, imprisoned by the Chinese Communists in 1950 said, 'How is it that so many saints down the ages have been able to live in triumph behind bars? It is because they have discovered the secret of freedom. It is the conscious co-operation with the Living God in the fulfilment of the pure design for which he made us.' Let's make that our aim too.

1:21–26
Nothing is more remarkable than the Christian confrontation with death. Here the question is raised: Death – *is it a plus or a minus?*

Here we have:

- vindication after death
- victory over death
- valuation of death.

The New Testament attitude to death is extraordinary. Paul looks death in the face and confronts the ultimate question: '*Will death add to you or only take away?*' Paul's answer is clear: 'To me to live is Christ, to die is gain.' For those for whom living means Christ, death will only gain us more of Him!

Our Christian forebears looked death full in the face. William Grimshaw, so mightily used of God in the eighteenth-century revival, pledged as a young man, to think of his own death every day of his life.

Dostoevsky's novels have such depth partly because he faced and survived an execution squad. Imminence of death concentrates the mind wonderfully on what is vital.

As the adage goes: death is a terminal illness: if you don't deal with death it will kill you!

Paul's deliberations about whether to stay or go sound as if he's negotiating with God. But as John Eldredge has said, we must quit playing chess with God because we can never win. No, Paul is not bargaining with God here. Rather he is exercising the unique freedom of someone who, long ago, handed over complete control of his life and reputation to the Lord Jesus and is not now about to take it back!

To use the jargon of our business friends, Paul is in a 'win-win' situation. He can't lose because he is totally committed to Christ being magnified in his body whether by life or death.

Dietrich Bonhoeffer's last words before being killed by the Nazis were: 'This is the end; for me the beginning of life.'

In John Piper's words, 'When the future grace of dying in Christ takes hold of you, it frees you from fear and gives courage to live the most radical self-sacrificing life of love.'

1:27–30 Living lives worthy of the gospel

[27]Whatever happens, conduct yourselves in a manner worthy of the gospel of Christ. Then, whether I come and see you or only hear about you in my absence, I will know that you stand firm in one spirit, contending as one man for the faith of the gospel [28]without being frightened in any way by those who oppose you. This is a sign to them that they will be destroyed, but that you will be saved – and that by God. [29]For it has been granted to you on behalf of Christ not only to believe on him, but also to suffer for him, [30]since you are going through the same struggle you saw I had, and now hear that I still have.

Just as Paul read his circumstances in the perspective of the gospel so now he urges the Philippians to make the same gospel the pattern on which to base their lives. The imperative 'Live your lives …' or 'Let your conduct be …' uses a unique political verb which means 'live as citizens of a kingdom'.

Anticipating 3:20, Paul gives here the Christian Citizens Charter. The gospel of Jesus is not only good news to be received and believed but has the power to shape our behaviour and lifestyle.

Conduct 'worthy of the gospel' is characterised especially by a serious commitment to Christian *unity*: 'standing firm in one spirit' as if in warfare; 'striving together' for the faith of the gospel as if in an athletic contest. Disunity in the Church still mars our witness to the gospel. If only we could remember that we are committed to a common cause as citizens of the same city, athletes playing in the same team, soldiers fighting on the same side. Unity would make us fearless in the face of any opposition. This was exactly what Paul was urging the Philippians to understand in their situation of social harassment and economic hardship. The increasing conflict that is coming to the Church will surely test how united we are but will expose the difference between those who are perishing and those who are being saved. We shall count it as a privilege to be found worthy to suffer for the sake of the gospel as Paul did.

Paul has just emphasised how vital is unity in the face of all that opposes the Christian gospel and the Christian Church; so 2:1–4.

2:1–4 Have a Christian mindset

¹If you have any encouragement from being united with Christ, if any comfort from his love, if any fellowship with the Spirit, if any tenderness and compassion, ²then make my joy complete by being like-minded, having the same love, being one in spirit and purpose. ³Do nothing out of selfish ambition or vain conceit, but in humility consider others better than yourselves. ⁴Each of you should look not only to your own interests, but also to the interests of others.

Paul continues his plea for Christian unity.

All four of his exhortations are about the life Christians have *in common*.

Paul expects the Philippians to *think alike*, to have what is nowadays called a 'mindset' which shows common allegiances and loyalties.

He wants them also to show the *same love* for one another, and to share the same feelings and attitudes of those whose lives have been bound together in *common accord*.

Lastly he urges on them a *common interest*, so that in their aims and goals they are as 'one mind'.

Only changed people can unite like this. It requires that we humbly set aside personal vanity and rivalry. In fame-conscious times, humility is an out-of-fashion virtue. In a culture which urges positive self-esteem, humility is a key suspect in the psychological crime of 'beating yourself up'. But if we learn humility by taking the yoke of Jesus and bearing the fruit of His Spirit, this virtue, far from being demeaning, is a diamond facet in being truly human.

In this light, humility is not the negative reaction of denigrating yourself but the positive willingness to consider others better than yourself. In the community of the cross, self-interest is put to death and we learn the new skills of seeing things from other people's point of view. But who lives in a house like this? Only those who have tasted the consolation of Christ, who abide in the comfort of God's love and who enjoy the fellowship of the Holy Spirit. We can surely detect in Paul's thinking here an underlying Trinitarian consciousness. Believers in Christ have been embraced by God's Trinity life, drawn into the divine relationship of harmony and loving interchange. By grace this is the measure and the power of our own life together as believers.

This is the *Christian mindset* – to employ a modern way of speaking.

And 'mindset' is an accurate term here. Paul is as usual concerned for the Christian 'mind' urging that we renew our way of thinking and begin to learn abiding habits of thinking which shape our attitudes to one another.

Nothing is more important than developing a settled, intelligent, biblical, Christ-centred, cruciform mindset.

The humility of the Lord Jesus is a wonder to behold! He humbles Himself in becoming fully one of us and as a young man submits to His earthly parents in Nazareth where He is apprenticed to the carpenter's trade.

He asserts no rights but submits to the baptism of John in order to fulfil all righteousness.

He claims no inherent powers, only the power of the indwelling Spirit of God which came upon Him at the Jordan.

He lives a humbly God-dependent life of prayer and fasting.

He is not on 'automatic-pilot' but lives by faith and finds His way by groping, bending His will to the revealed Word of Scripture and listening for the Father's voice.

He sets out determinedly not to initiate His own campaign but to accomplish His Father's objectives.

He proudly consorts with outcasts, welcomes children and is honoured to be in the presence of women, but is unimpressed with displays of power or piety.

He walks humbly with His God, loves mercy and does justice as God's faithful covenant partner.

His is truly a servant Kingship. Whether entering His royal city on a humble donkey rather than a grand war-horse or bending to wash His disciples' feet, He stoops to conquer our hearts.

In Gethsemane, wrestling with God's will, He trustingly takes the cup His Father gives Him.

Refusing to call on angel legions to save Him, He humbled Himself by becoming obedient unto death. Though armed with power to take up His life again He commits it to the safekeeping of His Father in sure and certain hope of the promised resurrection!

Let this mind be in you ...

Prayer and Reflection

Lord, it is so good to know that nothing can stop the progress
of the gospel.
Neither the failures of Your friends nor the fury of Your enemies
has been able to stand in its way.
Thank You that through all the ups and downs of Christian
history, the gospel has come down to us as the power of God
unto salvation.
Your love is so tenacious Lord; it penetrates closed doors and
will not let us go until it has blessed us.
I take heart from the example left by Your apostles and martyrs
and saints who stayed faithful to You in all circumstances.
Thank You for stirring Paul to be bold in prison, and John to
see visions on Patmos.
Above all I thank You for Jesus who has changed everything.
In His light life is different, death is different.
I reach out in faith to Your future, Lord, to the light that shines
beyond death in the sure and certain hope of resurrection.

- Write a letter to a sympathetic non-Christian friend who has
  asked you to explain the Christian view of death and
  resurrection

- Revisit a time of great difficulty in your life and recall how 'the
  prayers of the saints' and 'the supply of the Spirit' enabled you
  to come through.

- What is your 'prison cell'? Within what limits and under what
  constraints do you need to ask Jesus to help you today?

PHILIPPIANS

2:5–11 **The mindset of Jesus**

- the historic story of Jesus
- the true story of Adam
- the fulfilled story of Israel
- the astonishing story of God!
- the revised story of the world

2:5-11

⁵Your attitude should be the same as that of Christ Jesus:

⁶Who, being in very nature God,
    did not consider equality with God something to be grasped,
⁷but made himself nothing,
    taking the very nature of a servant,
    being made in human likeness.
⁸And being found in appearance as a man,
    he humbled himself
    and became obedient to death – even death on a cross!
⁹Therefore God exalted him to the highest place
    and gave him the name that is above every name,
¹⁰that at the name of Jesus every knee should bow,
    in heaven and on earth and under the earth,
¹¹and every tongue confess that Jesus Christ is Lord,
    to the glory of God the Father.

'The parabola of redemption':

(A) 'equal with God' (v.6)	equal honours as 'Lord' (v.11)
(B) 'human one ...'(v.7)	exalted to truly human position (v.10)
(C) humbled one (v.8)	humiliation turned to exaltation (v.9)

result   **CROSS**   reason for

2:5–11 The mindset of Jesus

This wonderful passage tells a number of stories as one story.[16]

1. At one level it is of course the *story of Jesus*.
No one exhibits this unself-regarding better than the Lord Jesus Himself. Paul celebrates the example of Jesus in what some scholars consider an early Christian hymn and urges the Philippians to let this mind be in them which was also in Him. Their model is nothing less than the incarnation of the eternal Son of God! Their model is the One who was 'in the form of God' and shared the very nature of God. But if we ask what His attitude to this 'equality with God' was, our English translations offer: 'He did not consider it robbery to be equal with God' (NKJV) or 'something to be grasped' (NIV).

Recent scholarship has wrestled with the meaning of the contentious word '*harpagmon*'. Should this read 'something one does not yet have but is seeking to grasp or snatch'? Or should it read, as Roy Hoover argued – increasingly backed by others, notably N.T. Wright in his exhaustive analysis of this passage – that '*harpagmon*' refers to '*what someone already has but chooses not to exploit or take advantage of*'. The NRSV is to be preferred here because it is the first major translation to reflect these, by now, well-accepted findings and to speak of Christ Jesus,

> … who, though he was in the form of God,
>> did not regard equality with God
>> as something to be exploited,
> but emptied himself,
>> taking the form of a slave,
>> being born in human likeness.
> And being found in human form,
>> he humbled himself

and became obedient to the point of death –
even death on a cross.

Therefore God also highly exalted him
  and gave him the name
  that is above every name,
so that at the name of Jesus
  every knee should bend,
  in heaven and on earth and under the earth,
and every tongue should confess
  that Jesus Christ is Lord,
  to the glory of God the Father. (NRSV)

I am labouring this point but it is the best way of reading the text and has considerable implications. Christ exists in the 'form of God' (*en morphē*, Gk.).

But 'Christ did not consider his equality with God as something to take advantage of …' This implies that 'being equal with God' and 'being in the form of God' – whatever distinction we might make between them – do not refer to anything less than full-scale divinity and the honours pertaining to that state.[17]

In other words, Christ refused to exploit to His own advantage a position He already had.

That is, 'nothing described as "being equal with God" or "in the form of God" is being given up; rather it is re-interpreted, understood in a manner in striking contrast to what one might have expected'.[18]

In other words, in contrast to oriental despots, Jesus understood His position to mean self-negation – not self-aggrandisement – the vocation described in verses 7–8.

Without ceasing to be what He was, the Lord Jesus did not take advantage of His exalted position, He did not exploit it for His own selfish purposes. When He came among us He did not dazzle us with displays of overwhelming divine power nor did He intimidate us with bullying tactics. He never acted in possessive or exploitative ways. He was secure enough and humble enough to look us in the eye and meet us at our own level.

2:7 '... emptied himself'

This phrase has to be handled carefully lest it lead us down the cul-de-sac of asking 'emptied of what?'

This was the road taken by so-called 'kenotic Christologies'.

The answer which is usually supplied is in terms of omnipotence and omniscience. But Paul is not talking of the loss or laying aside of divine attributes but of the 'rendering of something powerless', or emptying it of apparent significance (cf. Rom. 4:14; 1 Cor. 1:17; 9:15).

He 'made himself of no reputation' is not far short of the mark or, even better, 'he poured himself out'.

Paul is celebrating the utter self-giving of God in Christ. When he looks at Jesus from manger to cross, Paul sees a life poured out in lavish self-expenditure for the sake of others. The one glorious pre-incarnate life of God poured itself into a human life at Bethlehem and poured out in sacrificial death at Easter. We can perhaps hear an echo of Isaiah 53:12 where the servant of the Lord 'poured out his soul unto death'. It was, wrote P.T. Forsyth, 'as if the limpid waters that transfigure every stream, ran off to leave only the muddy debris of death.'[19] His life and death taxed His deepest inner resources. For the sake of us prodigals our Eldest Brother entered the far country of rebellion and death and squandered His life in righteous living and redemptive dying. Thank God He did.

2. But then again this story is told, by way of contrast, as the *true story of Adam, our human story*.

Jesus here is shown moving in the opposite direction to Adam.

Adam, made in the image of God, grasped at being equal with God – a status which was not his to have. By contrast, Jesus, the image of God as the Last Adam, refused to cling onto His divine status but voluntarily renounced a status He had every right to.

Where Adam in pride sought to become like God, Christ in humility becomes human. His is the truly human life. And it achieves as its true end that destiny always envisaged for Adam's sons – that of being co-regent with God, exercising dominion as Lord over the world.

Often the incarnation is regarded as a 'category mistake'. That is, it is assumed that being God and being human are inherently incompatible states. But if we think that it is impossible for God to become human – that's just what He did!

Genesis 1:26–28 shows an essential compatibility between God and the human creatures He has made in His image. It follows that there is a certain appropriateness about God coming in human form in incarnation. It is as if our humanness is a vehicle designed from the beginning as a means of God's self-expression. God called humans to be the sovereign-wise rulers of this world so that He might Himself become the sovereign-wise Ruler of the world by becoming human Himself!

This story, as we shall see, is the only authentic and truly human story there is – the one which fulfils every human potential to the glory of the Father.

3. The story told here is also telling of the strange but climactic fulfilment of *the story of Israel*.

Called out of slavery to be God's servant partner for the salvation of the world, but refusing the way of humility and obedience, Israel opted for wilful disobedience.

As a result Israel plunged down into the 'ignominious death' of exile, ending up ironically and tragically enslaved again in the very place from which Abraham had first come at the beginning of her story.

As Israel's Messiah, Jesus re-runs the Israel story successfully. He particularly moulds Himself to that concentrated part of the story told in Isaiah 40–55, of God's agent whose humble servanthood and

REJOICE! THE KING IS LORD

willing obedience to death brings salvation to the world. How Israel's story might look if it passed through the prism of Christ's humble death and triumphant vindication is told in the parallel story of Paul in 3:1–21.

Membership of God's true covenant people means precisely living out this story and no other. As a result we have a different story.

It involves not being obsessed with acquiring status and glory or acting in self-regarding or exploitative ways but exhibits the selfless, other-regarding humility, born in those who have been immersed by faith-baptism into the story of this dying and rising Jesus.

4. And then again what is truly remarkable is that Paul is telling this story as the *story of God*!

What does Godship look like? What does it look like to be a god and to behave like one? *The truth of Christology is a truth about God; just as the truth of the Trinity is a truth about Jesus* (Stephen Neill).

Telling the story of Jesus like this is a way of telling the story of the one true God!

'The real humiliation of the incarnation and the Cross is that one who was himself God, and who never during that whole process stopped being God, could embrace such a vocation' (Tom Wright).

This is, therefore, the ultimate revelation of God. This story offers a radically new view of God. One might assume that to be God means to be pompous, high and mighty. It is quite the reverse according to this vision.

But if this is the definitive revelation of what it means to be 'equal with God' then a brilliant new light is thrown on God.

The climax in verse 11 confirms this. The quotation from Isaiah 45:23 which affirms Yahweh's name to be applicable to Jesus not only stamps Jesus as sharing the very Godness of God but gives an unmistakable divine endorsement to what 'being equal with God' really looks like – ie, it looks like this!

The vindication of Jesus is 'God's "yes" to *this* expression of "equality with God"'.

'The concern is with divine selflessness; God is not an acquisitive being, grasping and seizing, but self-giving for the sake of others'.[20]

In Christ, God has told His real autobiographical story. God is not a Being gripped with the lust to exploit His advantages; He is motivated not by the love of power but the power of love.

Here is the truth of Christology and theology and universal humanity wrapped up in a very particular Jewish story.

> Paul believed that in Jesus Christ the true nature of the living God had been revealed ultimately and finally. God is not a grasping, self-centred being, but is most truly known through the one who, himself in the form of God and thus equal with God, poured out himself in sacrificial love by taking the lowest place, the role of a slave, whose love for his human creatures found its consummate expression in his death on the cross. That this is God's own nature and doing has been attested for all time by Christ Jesus' divine vindication; he has been exalted by God to the highest place by having been given the name of God himself; the Lord is none other than Jesus Christ.[21]

Written in this way, 'the parabola of redemption' exhibits, as nothing else does, the full and final glory of God (v.11c) so that we see God in His full colours.

5. Finally, what is being told here – by contrast – is the *story of the world* – in particular the story of the world Paul knew, the world of Roman Imperial power and might and that world is being subverted!

Jesus Christ is the Last Emperor.

For the early Christians Jesus was the Jewish 'Messiah', 'the

Christ'. Old Testament prophetic voices like Psalm 2 had declared God's intention to make His king in Jerusalem eventually Lord of the whole world. Peter announced on the Day of Pentecost that as a result of Easter that was exactly what God had done to Jesus. Paul is singing from the same hymn-sheet when he declares that, as a result of His obedience unto the death of the cross, Jesus has been exalted and given the name above every name. This name, in context, can only be 'Lord' – the very name applied in the Greek Old Testament to God Himself (Isa. 45:23–24)! When Jesus is announced then all must bow the knee and confess that 'He is Lord'.

Needless to say this subverts the values of our godless contemporary world just as it turned upside down the world Paul and the Philippians knew at first hand – the world of Imperial Roman power and authority. Caesar's empire – and every empire since – is a parody of the real thing!

While Paul wrote, the Caesars were annexing to themselves the title '*kurios*' or 'Lord'. Nowhere outside of Rome would this have been felt more keenly than in the Roman colony of Philippi. But the Christians there had heard and believed a different script in which Jesus, not Caesar, is Lord of the world. No wonder so many of the first apostles ended up in prison or that so many Christians now as then give their lives for Jesus.

Rejoice this King *is* Lord!

Prayer and Reflection

Father, as I have reflected again on the story of Jesus, I am
    amazed at this revelation of Your self-giving love.
Jesus, Son of God, thank You for not exploiting Your advantages
    for selfish ends.
Jesus, Lord of Glory, thank You for humbling Yourself and
    bending so low.
Jesus, Master and Commander, thank You for becoming an
    obedient servant for us.
Jesus, Lord of Life, thank You for dying our death for us.

I bow my knee before You, Lord, and wonder at the God I meet
    in You.
By Your Spirit, help me in dying to myself to rise up in newness
    of life.
Renew my mind so that, in Him, His mindset may be mine too.
For the sake of Your kingdom,
Amen.

- How might the 'parabola of redemption' in the career of Jesus
  alter the way we think about the way we
    - relate to each other as Christians?
    - define power and success in politics and business?
    - understand what God is like?

- 'Creeds are best sung not signed' – do you agree, and why?

PHILIPPIANS

2:5–11 Reviewed

Let's review what Paul has just been saying in this extraordinary and memorable passage. Whether or not it is an early Christian hymn, it is surely telling a story in a song.

This is *my* story,
this is my song …

Here, obviously, is the *story of Jesus*, God made flesh. But Jesus, let us not forget, is the Truly Human One and so we need to see in Him *our human story* too. In contrast to Adam who was made 'in the image of God' but grasped at being equal with God, this One, the One who was always with God did not exploit His advantage but humbled Himself to embrace our human condition. If you want to know what a truly human life looks like, look at Jesus. To be truly human is to walk the way of service, humility and obedience to God.

Even more remarkably the story being told here is *the story of God*! What does Godhood look like and how does it behave? The central mystery of the gospel is that the story of Jesus, the Truly Human One is the story of the One true God! It gives us a wholly new way of looking at God. God is not a high-and-mighty Being, grandiose and self-serving. Quite the reverse. Humility and willingness to suffer for others is the stuff of divinity. The climax confirms this. That God's own unique name of 'Lord' is applied to Jesus not only confirms the very Godness of Jesus but also gives an ultimate divine endorsement to what 'being equal with God' means. Jesus is the autobiography of God. How amazing! This is really *the* Story and *the* Song to sing!

Now 2:12ff. 'therefore' … how is this to be worked out in practical living and behaving.

2:12–18 Working out your salvation

[12]Therefore, my dear friends, as you have always obeyed – not only in my presence, but now much more in my absence – continue to work out your salvation with fear and trembling, [13]for it is God who works in you to will and to act according to his good purpose.

[14]Do everything without complaining or arguing, [15]so that you may become blameless and pure, children of God without fault in a crooked and depraved generation, in which you shine like stars in the universe [16]as you hold out the word of life – in order that I may boast on the day of Christ that I did not run or labour for nothing. [17]But even if I am being poured out like a drink offering on the sacrifice and service coming from your faith, I am glad and rejoice with all of you. [18]So you too should be glad and rejoice with me.

2:12–13 Spiritual work-out

The stunning picture of Jesus Paul has just painted comes with a 'therefore' attached, calling us to respond. We do so not simply by drawing a logical conclusion or even by following an example but by being *connected to a power which changes our life.*

We must 'work out' what is ours. Of course, there is no hint that we can achieve our own salvation. Salvation is God's gift. But we are urged to 'work out our salvation' in the sense of living out the life we possess in Christ.

Passivity is not an option for us. The kind of attitude which complacently says, 'let go and let God' will not do. We must co-operate with the power of God working in us.

Deep within the springs of each Christian's personality, God is at work, re-directing our wills and rejuvenating our motivation to do His will!

This is the glorious reality of the new covenant life once promised by Israel's prophets and now made good by the Holy Spirit (see Jer. 31:31ff.; Ezek. 36). So, next time you hear your inner self saying: 'I can't do God's will, I'm too weak. I keep failing', give this answer to your wavering heart and let God's Word reverberate within your soul: 'I am working actively inside you to will and to work what pleases Me ... I am continuing the good work I began in you and will bring it to completion ...'

How awesome! Perhaps we should stick a label on every Christian: 'Danger – God at work!' No wonder Paul reacts with 'fear and trembling', not because he has a nervous disposition, but at the breathtaking thought that the mighty Creator God is working in and through him.

2:14–16 Stars in *His* eyes

We live in a media-saturated world where celebrities are famous merely for being famous. But there are no 'stars' in that sense in God's earthly firmament.

To be a star in God's eyes demands no heroic exploits except the major feats of not grumbling or complaining! Is that all, we may ask? But, be honest, how many churches would be transformed if we stopped griping and disputing among ourselves.

Even more serious is to grumble in front of unbelievers for this, as Oswald Chambers pointed out, is to cast a slur on the reputation of God!

If we now return to the text and dig beneath the surface, we may detect significant Old Testament references. Paul's words seem clearly to echo the tiresome attitude of the children of Israel in the wilderness, which so severely put God to the test (Num. 14:27; 16:41; 17:5,10, cf. 1 Cor. 10:10). But, as Daniel hoped, one day the 'righteous will shine like the stars' (Dan. 12:3).

The darkness in which the stars appear is defined as the 'perverse and crooked generation' – a term once applied to a rebellious Israel (Deut. 32:5, NKJV) – now ironically applied to the society in which the Philippians are called to shine.

As Christians we can trace a continuity with the people of God in Old Testament times. Their story is meant to challenge us to live with uncomplaining patience and to hold firm the Word of Life by believing and testifying to its truth.

The famous novelist, Robert Louis Stevenson, recalls how one evening as a child he stood transfixed at his nursery window watching the lamplighter in the street. When his nanny asked the boy what he was doing, he replied: 'I'm watching the man knocking holes in the darkness.'

2:17–18 Sacrificial offering

The language of 'sacrifice' that Paul uses here has not worn well in recent times. After two World Wars in which profligate waste of human lives was officially and perhaps too glibly justified as 'noble sacrifice', many modern people, for whom no cause seems worth dying for, are wary of the whole notion. But it is undeniably a vital theme of biblical faith.

Paul often reaches back into the Levitical tradition in Israel to describe Christian ministry. To Timothy, for example, he speaks of being 'poured out like a drink offering', a reference to the outpouring of wine that accompanied, and in some sense rounded off, the daily burnt offerings and grain offerings (2 Tim. 4:6). The same imagery is employed here. Paul recognises that the ministry God has given him exhausts his energies and entails suffering. But this 'sacrifice' is not dragged from him reluctantly but is part of his willing and joyful self-offering in the cause of the gospel.

Even more remarkably, he turns matters on their heads by telling the Philippians that *his* outpouring of life is a drink offering that climaxes *their* sacrifice, not his! They can therefore rejoice in each other's plight. Extraordinary isn't it? The courageous self-offering of apostles and martyrs is only the crowning seal of value placed on your faith as Christ's people. It was said of Bishop J.C. Ryle that he woke each morning and thought of his bed as an altar, so dedicating himself as a living sacrifice to God each day.

2:19–30 Unsung heroes

Timothy and Epaphroditus

[19]I hope in the Lord Jesus to send Timothy to you soon, that I also may be cheered when I receive news about you. [20]I have no-one else like him, who takes a genuine interest in your welfare. [21]For everyone looks out for his own interests, not those of Jesus Christ. [22]But you know that Timothy has proved himself, because as a son with his father he has served with me in the work of the gospel. [23]I hope, therefore, to send him as soon as I see how things go with me. [24]And I am confident in the Lord that I myself will come soon.

[25]But I think it is necessary to send back to you Epaphroditus, my brother, fellow-worker and fellow-soldier, who is also your messenger, whom you sent to take care of my needs. [26]For he longs for all of you and is distressed because you heard he was ill. [27]Indeed he was ill, and almost died. But God had mercy on him, and not on him only but also on me, to spare me sorrow upon sorrow. [28]Therefore I am all the more eager to send him, so that when you see him again you may be glad and I may have less anxiety. [29]Welcome him in the Lord with great joy, and honour men like him, [30]because he almost died for the work of Christ, risking his life to make up for the help you could not give me.

How intriguingly does the Bible mix the sublime and the mundane. Isn't it extraordinary how the jottings of some ancient travel plans from long ago, such as we have here, end up in Holy Scripture?

This, of course, is just part of the genius of the gospel which sanctifies the mundane and makes the ordinary sublime. Timothy will arrive at Philippi soon, while Epaphroditus is coming later; of such is the kingdom of heaven. You see, the Christian story is not all about great names and great feats.

I find it immensely heartening that some of the apostles of Jesus rate only half a line of Scripture while these two 'saints in ordinary' rate half a chapter!

Equally heart-warming is the reminder that the great apostle was no lone-wolf but gathered men around him who were friends not functionaries. Timothy and Epaphroditus are two of the gospel's countless 'unsung heroes'. For his part, Timothy is presented to the Philippians as a role-model who seeks the interests of others rather than his own and is as near to a son as Paul ever had.

Epaphroditus's story is a heart-warmingly human one. He is evidently missing home and worrying how the Philippians might be reacting to news of his illness. How very human! Welcome him back, says Paul; don't think he has let you down by returning; in fact he risked his neck for me.

All in all this is a wonderful sample of how redemption transfigures everyday events and the Holy Spirit inspires a practical down-to-earth spirituality. Who you are, what you are doing and even where you are going today, matters to the Lord.

Prayer and Reflection

Once again, Lord, I find the thought of You working deep within
me mysterious and wonderful.

There is so much to regret; so much I still long to be and
achieve.
Forgive me for contributing my share to the stack of complaints
You receive.
Go on saving me from the self-pity that casts aspersions on Your
character and doubts upon Your reputation for treating Your
people well.
Help me to listen to Your Spirit's voice and to draw on His
power.
Teach me to forgo my headstrong illusions and to focus on Your
goals for my life.
Stir me to reach out for Your future with a spirit of adventure so
that I may trust and travel with You every day with joy.
Amen.

- Recall the name and stories of 'unsung heroes' of the faith –
parents, friends, school teachers, work-colleagues, for instance
– whose example made a difference to your life in Christ.

- In the light of this section – 2:12–30 – describe what a
Christian is.

- In our media-conscious age, reflect on who your idols and
icons are. How might 2:5–30 redefine what it means to be a
star and a celebrity?

REVISED BALANCE SHEET

PHILIPPIANS

3:1–4a True and false worship

¹Finally, my brothers, rejoice in the Lord! It is no trouble for me to write the same things to you again, and it is a safeguard for you.

²Watch out for those dogs, those men who do evil, those mutilators of the flesh. ³For it is we who are the circumcision, we who worship by the Spirit of God, who glory in Christ Jesus, and who put no confidence in the flesh – ⁴though I myself have reasons for such confidence.

3:1–2

We come to the first of two groups whom Paul sharply denounces in this chapter – probably different groups.

The matter is serious enough to draw some very tough talking from Paul. So sharp is his speech at this point that some scholars feel it clashes with the more benign overall tone of the letter and suggest it comes from another epistle. But, as we pointed out in the introduction, this is a misreading of Philippians and the situation addressed there. It is a mistake to read the situation as if it were all unclouded skies.

To be sure, Paul's words do not make for easy listening. In his passionate outburst some serious name-calling is going on: 'Watch out there are dogs about! They talk righteousness but do evil! If you let them cut your body they will mutilate your faith!'

So, who is this fierce talk aimed at and why?

As with the Galatians, it seems the Philippians are being troubled by some Jewish Christians who want to impose on Gentile Christians the specific marks of Jewishness – particularly circumcision. From Abraham onwards (Gen. 17), circumcision was the outward sign, in males at least, of being in God's covenant family. This 'identity marker' was especially important for Jews living outside the promised land, and was a contentious issue in the apostolic mission.

In such contexts, the term 'the circumcision' is shorthand for 'having the status of God's covenant people'.

We can feel the thrust of what Paul is saying here, if we pause to reflect on the fact that throughout the Old Testament, circumcision was always meant to signify a deeper 'circumcision of the heart' (Deut. 10:16; 30:6; Jer. 4:4; 9:25 cf. Rom. 2:28–29).

Above all, since Christ has come, circumcision, as a ritual act, no longer counts for anything in a believer's relationship with God (cf. Gal. 6:15). What matters is the reality of which it was a sign. Faith in Jesus Christ is now the only true 'identity marker' showing who are the covenant people of God. As far as Paul is concerned, to say otherwise is to threaten the freedom of the gospel of grace.

So, when so much is at stake, Paul does not mince his words. As a Jewish Christian, Paul had his own turbulent history with such false teachers and he has deep aversion to their message.

For Paul, faith in Christ is now the only indelible sign of being in God's covenant family. He reacts strongly to anything that says knowing Jesus is not enough and must be supplemented by special rites – strong feelings, then, and strong words, so precious is our freedom in Christ. Let's rejoice in Christ over this right now!

3:1-2

In fact it's worth noting that Paul prefaces his warning with encouragement. If we relish what we have and are in Christ then false teaching will inevitably have less appeal. It is when we begin to lose confidence in what God's grace has done and is doing in our lives that we become vulnerable to the lure of legalism as the way to bolster our defences and define our identity.

To 'rejoice in the Lord' is the surest way to avoid this snare. At this point we may find it hard to accept that we can be *commanded* to rejoice. In our therapeutic, touchy-feely age, we find it impossible to believe that anything we do can alter our feelings. We assume that we are at the mercy of our emotions, whether joy or sadness, which rise unbidden from within us. But this is not true biblical psychology. The call to rejoice echoes through the Bible from the Psalms onwards. Scripturally speaking, rejoicing is not so much a feeling as an activity, a release of praise and thanksgiving and song.

Many modern books on spirituality tend to imply that it is an 'introvert' business, dealing with what goes on in the depths, or talking of the inner journey. This is true as far as it goes, but the Bible also encourages what we might call an 'extravert' spirituality. We've all met the cheerless Christian who claims to be 'joyful on the inside' but does so through gritted teeth! No, joy is to be expressed, feelingly, lovingly and even physically.

We should take particular notice of the fact that Paul issues his call to 'rejoice' in the context of his severe warning about the danger of false teaching. This strongly suggests, as we have said, that the Philippians' best antidote to the 'legalisers' was for them to celebrate what they have in Christ. Joy in knowing Jesus as the Christ far outweighs any lingering attachment to pre-Christian securities however pious – even blameless Torah observance, an outmoded order of things that has no future in it. And his 'finally' does not so much indicate that Paul is uncertain when to finish but perhaps can be taken in the sense 'above all, rejoice' or 'in the end, rejoice …'

Paul always wants joy to be his final note …

3:3 Worship

Paul celebrates the fact that the Philippian Christians – whether Jewish or Gentile – are bone fide members of God's new covenant community. The trademark of physical circumcision operative from Abraham's day has become obsolete and the real 'circumcised ones' can now be defined as those who enjoy the privileges of the new covenant relationship promised by the prophets long ago.

Notice with appreciation how Paul spells this out.

The first characteristic is that we 'serve' or 'worship God in the Spirit'. This is the opposite to 'living in' or 'by the flesh'. Sometimes

Paul uses the term 'the flesh' to refer to what is bodily and physical. But usually, as here, he uses the term in a moral and spiritual sense. To live 'in the flesh' is to live centred on oneself and without God. In this case 'in the flesh' is particularly apt since the false teachers are those who are advocating circumcision which was a literal cut in the flesh! (They are scathingly described as 'mutilators of the flesh', v.2.)

On the other hand, to live 'in the Spirit' is to live a human life in all its aspects controlled and empowered by the Spirit of God. Furthermore, our worship is characterised by the way 'we boast in Christ Jesus'.

Trusting Christ and experiencing the Spirit are the only genuine signs of our being in God's covenant family.

Our trademark is that we exuberantly exult in the glory of the Person of Jesus Christ. And we do so by totally repudiating any confidence in the flesh. As Paul argues, our status before God and our relationship with God do not depend on any inherited patterns of privilege or achievements of our own piety but solely on Christ and the Spirit. We are in God's covenant family through grace. So let's make a song and dance about that!

3:4–16 Paul's story

Compare 3:4–21 with 2:5–11

Paul's description of his own story is clearly meant to mirror that of the humble and exalted Jesus in 2:5–11 and is to be seen as the inevitable outcome of a life lived in conjunction with that of such a Christ. Paul describes *'his own hope in terms of conformity to the emptying-death-resurrection paradigm of Christ's career'.*[22]

Note the verbal parallels:

2:3–11
The call is to 'humility'
(*'tapeinophrosunē'*)
not 'empty glory' (v.3)
but he took the way of humility
by 'humbling himself'
(*'etapdinōsen'*) to achieve
salvation and 'glory' (*'doxa'*)

existing in the *'morphē'* of God
taking the *'morphē'* of a slave 2:6–7

do not 'regard' or 'consider'
'ēgēsato' 2:6 (cf. 2:3)

found (*'euretheis'*) v.7
in 'appearance' (*'schēmati'*)

also compare:
obedient (*'hupēkoos'*)
unto death v.8

3:4–21
body of our
'humiliation'
(*'tapeinōseōs'*)
changed into
'conformity'
(*'summorphon'*)
with the body of
his glory (*'doxa'*)

(*'summorphizomenos'*)
  conformed to his death
  3:10 cf. 3:21

consider
  (*'ēgēmai'*)
  3:7,8,13

found (*'euretho'*) v.9
  (*'metaschēmatisei'*)
  transformed v.21

subject (*'hupotaxai'*)
all things – including
  death to himself v.21
  (cf. Psalm 8)

3:4b-6 Failed confidence

> If anyone else thinks he has reasons to put confidence in the flesh,
> I have more: ⁵circumcised on the eighth day, of the people of Israel,
> of the tribe of Benjamin, a Hebrew of Hebrews; in regard to the law,
> a Pharisee; ⁶as for zeal, persecuting the church; as for legalistic
> righteousness, faultless.

Let's begin to explore how Paul's autobiography mirrors the story of the humbled and exalted Jesus. What has happened to him, Paul tells us, is a model of what happens when one's life is joined through faith and baptism with the dying–rising career of Jesus.

Paul begins by confessing his failed confidence.

He does this first of all by rehearsing his impeccable pedigree as a long-standing member of God's elect. Paul was always conscious of the high honour of his Jewish heritage. From here and elsewhere in his writings, we learn that he loved the patriarchs, honoured the Torah, worshipped at Temple and synagogue, and soaked himself in the Hebrew Scriptures as the living oracles of the One Creator God. Clearly, he never denigrates these things in themselves and continued throughout his life in Christ to value them. What he does deprecate strongly is the *false confidence* he had once placed in them. This is what he does here.

It was to Paul always a matter of deep regret that his zeal for God's Law had intially led him to disparage Jesus' claim to Messiahship and to persecute the Church. But in all other respects, he could claim to be 'blameless' as far as the righteousness of the Law was concerned. Paul is not claiming to have been 'faultless' but without blame in that, even when he sinned, he had recourse to the Law's prescribed remedies.

Yet, he admits, his law-keeping has become distorted into his 'own righteousness'.

In one sense there is nothing wrong with Paul's past except – as

Gordon Fee puts it – his past has no future in it! Of course, there should have been, because all that Paul inherited as a faithful Jew was intended to lead somewhere, in fact to lead to the feet of Christ. Almost despite himself, this is precisely what has happened to Paul and he delights in it. Paul, for one, has found the rainbow of salvation at the end of the trail and sees absolutely no need to retrace his steps.

3:7–9 Revised balance sheet

[7]But whatever was to my profit I now consider loss for the sake of Christ. [8]What is more, I consider everything a loss compared to the surpassing greatness of knowing Christ Jesus my Lord, for whose sake I have lost all things. I consider them rubbish, that I may gain Christ [9]and be found in him, not having a righteousness of my own that comes from the law, but that which is through faith in Christ – the righteousness that comes from God and is by faith.

This has led Paul to draw up what has been called a 'revised balance sheet'! In this rich and famous passage, we dwell on several points.

Firstly, like an accountant examining his spiritual stocks, Paul draws up his profit and loss account. In his 'revised balance sheet', the apostle reveals that his old status and privileges did not, in any way, add up to the joys of salvation in Christ.

In fact all that was previously profitable to him he has decisively written off, consigning them to the 'rubbish dump'!

This is tough talk again from Paul, especially about things that were once so precious to him. But in his eyes, knowing Jesus surpasses everything else.

Secondly, it is worth noting how closely Paul's testimony mirrors the story told of Jesus in 2:5–11. Like his Lord, Paul too has renounced a privileged status, suffered loss and undergone humiliation. In other words, this is the cruciform (or 'cross-shaped') Christ-pattern worked out in the history of one Jewish man.

As such, Paul exemplifies the way all his fellow-Jews might go to fulfil their destiny and achieve their true identity. In this sense Paul embodies Israel's story – as it might have been and still could be – just as Jesus embodied the whole human story.

Thirdly, if we were to ask Paul 'Was it worth it?' he would surely reply with a resounding 'Yes!' Right now he has gained a relationship with Christ; in that decisive future he is sure he will be 'found in Christ' with covenant membership not guaranteed by Law but given by God to those who believe in Jesus. Could a man be any richer?

Fourthly, he has discovered a new way of *righteousness* (v.9).

The word (*'dikaiosunē'*) is often translated 'justification'. Here it probably also implies something like 'vindication'. So, those who are justified are those who are vindicated. In other words, those who are finally vindicated as God's true people are precisely those who take their stand with the crucified Messiah, Jesus.

That is, God's people are no longer – if ever – taking their stand with Torah or any of its works, like circumcision, but wholly and entirely and finally casting in their lot with the crucified and exalted servant of God, Jesus who has Himself been vindicated in resurrection and exaltation to the place of supreme lordship. They do this through their 'faith in Christ' alone (v.9) or – in line with modern scholarship – through putting their faith in the 'faith(fulness) of Christ'.

As a consequence, they too are vindicated or declared to be in the right relationship with God; that is, declared to be His covenant people.

Embracing this new-found reality in Christ cost Paul everything. He found that his privileges advantaged him nothing nor could he exploit his privileged status for any gain that accrued to him.

This humbled him and recalled him to Israel's original servant vocation. In embracing this, Paul obediently submitted to immersion in Messiah's humiliating death. But because Christ was raised and exalted to final vindication, Paul too looks forward to ultimate vindication in final resurrection.

3:10–11 Knowing Jesus

[10]I want to know Christ and the power of his resurrection and the fellowship of sharing in his sufferings, becoming like him in his death, [11]and so, somehow, to attain to the resurrection from the dead.

The extraordinary re-evaluation of his life which Paul has undergone has given him a completely new ambition. He wants above all to '*know Jesus*' more and more. But notice that knowing Jesus involves entering more and more deeply into an experience both of His risen power and His suffering death!

Paul looked back on 'knowing Jesus' as a price infinitely worth counting. He wrote in his journal, 'I died on the Damascus Road. My previous life bit the dust of that Eastern Road. All my intellectual and moral achievements gasped their final breath when I had that breathtaking encounter with Jesus, crucified and risen; the old me died and a new Paul arose as if from the dead.'

So when Paul speaks of knowing Christ more he is speaking out of an already profound and firsthand experience:

- of knowing Christ as a moral power penetrating to the depths of one's personality,
- of Christ as the dominating influence in his life,
- of Christ the living Lord giving him the surge of courage to face an angry mob,
- of Christ the captivating Saviour turning the moral effort of

a legal past into a life-stretching adventure with the
Holy Spirit,
- of Christ filling the wings of his abilities and ambitions.

No wonder he still wants 'to know him'!

Having been enrolled in the curriculum of Christ's sufferings,
Paul is willing, for the further joy set before him, to be a graduate
of the 'school of Calvary' whatever it costs.

3:10–11

We ponder further that to 'know Jesus' is to enter the *'fellowship of
his sufferings'*.

What an amazing and paradoxical statement. An ever-
increasing acquaintance with the Risen Jesus comes through
'holding shares in His sufferings'!

Now we can appreciate how becoming a follower of Jesus
involves a drastic re-investment of our life. Having written off all
his previous assets as a Pharisee, Paul has declared himself
bankrupt, gone into voluntary liquidation and is now resolved to
invest his life's capital in the ongoing sufferings of Christ!

Nothing could be more relevant to today's Church, especially
those over-triumphalist sections who shout the loudest.

The resurrection did not cancel out the cross, as if Jesus did all the
dying while we do all the triumphing. No! By raising Jesus from the
dead God endorsed the whole self-giving, servant lifestyle that
had taken Him to the cross. Consequently, if we enjoy the power
of His resurrection operating in us – and by the Spirit we certainly
do – then we must realise it is intended to empower us precisely to
enter into the fellowship of His sufferings in the real world. This
is what knowing Jesus means.

Notice again how the language of 2:5–11 is echoed here as Paul
talks of being 'conformed' to His death, shaped to the cruciform
pattern of the way it was with Jesus. Finally, as with Jesus, Paul

hopes to 'attain to the resurrection of the dead' which, as the prophets dreamed, is the way God ultimately vindicates His people and shows they are really His. So the way of the cross leads home; the way of death leads to life; the way down is the way up.

3:12–14 Pressing on

[12]Not that I have already obtained all this, or have already been made perfect, but I press on to take hold of that for which Christ Jesus took hold of me. [13]Brothers, I do not consider myself yet to have taken hold of it. But one thing I do: Forgetting what is behind and straining towards what is ahead, [14]I press on towards the goal to win the prize for which God has called me heavenwards in Christ Jesus.

Paul continues to give us vivid insights into his own spiritual progress. He makes two virtually parallel statements built around the metaphor of a race in which the central message, emphasised twice, is: 'I press on'. Paul brackets this intense sense of purpose with three disclaimers which give a realistic context for his aspirations:

- He has 'not' yet obtained,
- He has 'not yet' been made complete,
- He does 'not' consider himself to have taken hold of his final destiny.

Paul is under no illusions about the present life. He is 'betwixt and between'. He has gained Christ but there is so much more to know and receive that lies ahead in God's well-stocked future. But his eye is on that future as a goal to be reached.

Paul recalls how he was apprehended at the crime scene, by Jesus on the Damascus Road and now he presses on to 'take hold of that for which Christ took hold of him'.

Paul's career was turned completely in the other direction on the Damascus Road. Jesus now sets the agenda for what is important to Paul; God's purposes not Paul's plans matter most. The goal and the prize that await at the finishing tape – whatever way you look at them – can only be that ultimate experience of 'knowing Jesus' which he has already told us is his overriding ambition. May God help us to live at 'full stretch' for Him.

3:13 Focused living

Sporting enthusiasts of a certain vintage will never forget that memorable mile race at the Empire Games in Vancouver many years ago when John Landy, the Australian champion, looked back over his left shoulder to see where Roger Bannister was, only for Bannister to pass him on his right!

Paul's forward-looking attitude to life implies focused living. We can penetrate further into Paul's powerful testimony to his own spiritual desire by noticing his 'one thing I do'. If we are to make spiritual progress we must make our relationship with the Lord our priority and concentrate on the 'one thing needful'.

Søren Kierkegaard, that strange but prophetic nineteenth-century Dane, said that 'purity of heart is to will one thing'.

Dissipation of energy gets us nowhere in the spiritual walk. If we spread ourselves too thin, we cover very little. We are followers of Him who might have been jack of all spiritual trades but made himself Master of one: death.

Stanley Jones once wryly commented: 'Where Paul said "this one thing I do" the modern Church says "these 40 things we dabble in"'. But this need not be so. We can ask the Lord to help us regroup our scattered resources or, where appropriate, streamline our commitments. It is perfectly possible to become single-minded without being narrow-minded.

Kierkegaard ended his book, *Purity of Heart*, by praying that God would 'give to the intellect wisdom to comprehend that one thing … to the heart sincerely to receive this understanding … to the will purity to will only one thing … amid distractions to will one thing, in suffering patience to will one thing.'[23]

We might make a fresh start today in simplifying our cluttered lives by taking to heart Austen Farrer's advice: 'Do fewer things and do them better.'

3:13–14 Past landmarks

Paul's pressing on takes him further away from past landmarks. We should perhaps not make too much of a psychological meal of Paul's 'forgetting what lies behind' though it has often been done in sermons and seminars.

It's certainly true that we must never allow needless regrets or memories or failures or limited education or handicaps of birth to stop us pressing forward with Jesus. But it is unlikely that Paul is referring either to previous deprivations or even to his pre-Christian past which he has recently rehearsed.

When Paul uses the athletic imagery elsewhere it usually refers to his apostolic ministry. So the likely point at issue here is that Paul refuses to rest on past successes but concentrates on pressing on towards the goal. He wants to do this without distractions. So we need to keep the race metaphor simple. Whatever else you do, don't look back.

'Keep on keeping on' as my father used to say. As the great nineteenth-century scholar, J.B. Lightfoot, paraphrases: 'Do not mistake me, I hold the language of hope not of assurance … forgetting the landmarks already passed and straining every nerve and muscle in the onward race, I press forward toward the goal.'

In this way we are invited to turn the landmarks into signposts to the future – the prize of the upward call of God in Christ Jesus.

Listen to Os Guinness:

Personally summoned by the Creator of the universe, we are given a meaning in what we do that flames over every second and inch of our lives. Challenged, inspired, rebuked, and encouraged by God's call we cannot for a moment settle down to the comfortable, the mediocre, the banal, and the boring. The call is always to the higher, the deeper, and the farther ...

In short, every time the marsh gas of sloth rises from the swamps of modern life, and threatens to overcome us, the call of God jerks us wide awake. Against the most sluggish temptation to feel 'who cares?' calling is the supreme motivation, the ultimate 'why'. God has called us, and we are never more ourselves than when we are fully stretched in answering. There is no yawning in response to this call.[24]

Prayer and Reflection

Father God, I relish the joy of worshipping You as a member
   of Your covenant family.
I boast only in Christ Jesus as my Lord and Saviour and put
   no confidence in my heritage or history or achievements.
Thank You, Holy Spirit, for making such worship possible.
So, Father, forgive me for looking elsewhere for reassurance
   about who I am.
Help me not to allow money or possessions or status or work
   or education or success – or lack of any or all of these
      things – to define who I am.
Knowing Jesus, I confess, is better than anything and makes
   everything better than it would otherwise be.
'Jesus, all for Jesus,
All I am and have and ever hope to be
All of my ambitions, hopes and plans,
I surrender them into your hands.'
Amen.

- Who sets the standard of living in your society and how does
  Paul's testimony affect your view of it?

- Draw up your own balance sheet of benefits and costs as a
  follower of Jesus Christ and acknowledge again what knowing
  Him is worth.

- 'The resurrection did not cancel out the cross, but endorsed it
  as the only truly human way to live.' Reflect on the truth of this
  statement and its implications for you and your fellow
  believers.

PHILIPPIANS

3:15–17   Be mature

3:18-21   **Natives and resident aliens!**
    enemies of the cross 3:18
    – dead ends 3:19
    colony of heaven 3:20
    – resurrection future 3:21

3:15-17 Be mature

¹⁵All of us who are mature should take such a view of things. And if on some point you think differently, that too God will make clear to you. ¹⁶Only let us live up to what we have already attained.

¹⁷Join with others in following my example, brothers, and take note of those who live according to the pattern we gave you.

Paul now urges his readers to be mature by sharing the 'view of things' he has just described. (His exhortation to 'have this mind' deliberately recalls 2:5 where he urged the Philippians to 'have the attitude [mind] of Christ'.)

Let's recall the characteristics of this mature point of view:

An unwavering commitment to knowing Jesus Christ. And as Douglas Webster has said, 'Knowing Jesus involves a personal encounter, an exclusive relationship, a permanent union, and a transformed life'.[25] That's enough to occupy two lifetimes!

A realistic appraisal of our own progress. 'I have not yet attained.' Discerning the New Testament's creative tension between what we have 'now' and what we hope for but do 'not yet' have, is the beginning of spiritual wisdom.

An unsentimental attitude to the past. We learn to forget – not by failing to recall God's mercies or benefits however they have come – but in the sense of not being paralysed by memory of failures or nostalgia for past securities.

An undiminished desire for God, what hymnwriter H.W. Faber called 'a jubilant pining and longing for God'.

An undistracted focus on the things that really matter so that we do fewer things better.

An unabashed tendency to be forward-looking. Paul's eyes were always on the coming Day and coming Saviour, on the End, the prize, the goal, so that he was not anchored to the past but drawn irresistibly onwards by the magnet of God's future.

But Paul recognises that there are different levels of maturity (3:15–16).

Meeting recently with men I trained with for ministry over 35 years ago, they could be divided into two groups: the world-weary, resigned and virtually retired, and those who have retained their zest, their eagerness for new adventures, their keen sense of calling. Many were still keen to keep pressing on. Are you?

Even in the best churches, we will inevitably meet varied levels of spiritual maturity in other people. Within the bonds of fellowship, Paul insists we can cope with this, without disparaging or patronising the less spiritually mature. In fact, he says, we can trust God together that He will open everyone's eyes to see from the same point of view. God can bring everyone 'up to speed' as it were, so that the progress of the many is not dragged back by the slowest member to a 'lowest common denominator'. What matters is that at whatever stage we are, we are still moving, still hungry for more of God.

Within a Christian atmosphere of mutual respect, there is room for a growing understanding of many issues, though not, for Paul, the issue of the cruciform life or the zealous pursuit of the upward call of God. These are non-negotiable. The bottom line is simple: 'Live up to the light you have received'. That is all that we can expect of anyone, including ourselves.

But what we have received in Christ is so life-changing that none of us ought to become apathetic or complacent, but inspired to a vigorous pursuit of God. As Duncan Campbell said, 'Let's not settle for anything less than heaven wills to give us'.

3:17

In fact, Paul is willing to be put forward as a model for mature and cruciform living: 'imitate me.'

At first glance, the idea of imitating Paul sounds as daunting as it does attractive. For me, it's the sheer intensity of Paul's approach to living which is both intimidating and impressive. But then we modern Christians have been too easily lulled into thinking that our faith is there to construct comfort-zones for us into which we can snuggle, protected from a dangerous world. Too often we simply want to be cosseted and stroked in a relaxed atmosphere.

All of which is a far cry from apostolic Christianity, where faith was bracing and life a challenge. It requires – and God provides – effort and energy and determination. We may only get splinters from the cross but that is, after all, what we told to carry.

We are not expected to emulate Paul's gifts or achievements but we are challenged to imitate his fervent concentration on the one thing worth doing with our life. And not Paul only but equally all who live the cruciform life and set the standard for the rest.

No wonder Oswald Chambers, reflecting on Paul's determination, was led to speak of giving 'my utmost for his highest'. Of Chambers himself, Raymond Edman once said: 'Never content with low attainment … he was always climbing the mountain peaks.'

When the British mountaineers, George Mallory and Andrew Irvine, were lost from sight near the summit of Everest in 1924, their companions beneath them reported to base camp that they were '*last seen still climbing*'. May that be true of us all.

3:18–21 Natives and resident aliens

[18]For, as I have often told you before and now say again even with tears, many live as enemies of the cross of Christ. [19]Their destiny is

destruction, their god is their stomach, and their glory is in their shame. Their mind is on earthly things. [20]But our citizenship is in heaven. And we eagerly await a Saviour from there, the Lord Jesus Christ, [21]who, by the power that enables him to bring everything under his control, will transform our lowly bodies so that they will be like his glorious body.

Now we come to one of the few polemical sections in the letter, where Paul speaks strongly of those he calls 'enemies of the cross'.

He turns from the example of those who are running his kind of race to warn the Philippians of those who are decidedly on another path altogether.

It's hard to know just who these people were whom Paul calls 'enemies of the cross'. It is unlikely that they are to be identified with 'the dogs' of verse 2 – they are almost certainly fellow Christians of one sort or another! But why the dreadful description?

Perhaps these people, like some in Corinth, were engaging in gluttonous binges and shameful sexual conduct, falsely believing that such physical appetites could be indulged without damage to their spiritual wisdom and power. Or perhaps they were simply opting for an easy-going version of the gospel, which had immediately apparent glitzy effects, rather than embracing the full-blooded gospel which committed them to a long-haul discipleship, marked by the cross as the path to ultimate glory.

Neither the script of Christ's story of humble and self-giving servanthood nor that of Paul's renunciation of all things for Christ's sake has any role for self-seeking stardom.

One thing is sure, it's very sobering indeed to realise that anyone believing in Jesus Christ might become enemies of His cross. Douglas Webster frames Paul's solemn warning this way, by saying that 'We may have all the right words, and be an expert on the doctrine of the Atonement, but if we do not share in his sufferings, "becoming like him in his death" (Phil. 3:10), we reject the cross'.[26]

Although Paul uses strong language to warn of the twisted truth these 'enemies of the cross' exemplify, he weeps for them at the same time. These are the only tears in the letter of joy, showing that he is torn apart by the thought of Christians living like pagans. Tragically turning all moral values and standards on their heads, they are indulging their physical appetites, 'idolising their bellies' in the process! What they delight in is what Paul considers they should be ashamed of.

As before in this letter, Paul targets the 'mindset' behind such behaviour. Their failure is that they 'set their minds on earthly things'. 'Earthly things' in this context are not the practical affairs of everyday life but things that characterise a worldly outlook which is in opposition to God. Elsewhere in Paul's writings, these include sexual immorality, impurity, greed, slander and factiousness. In other words an 'earthbound mindset' will involve both personal sins and those social sins which destroy unity and community in the Church. Who shapes your thinking is crucial. Paul has commended the mindset of Jesus as the only authentic criterion of a godly and truly human life. To be otherwise-minded is to court destruction. To abandon the cross is to forfeit the future inheritance. The narrow way of following Jesus, not the broad way of following social trends, leads to life.

3:20

In stark contrast to those whose horizon is limited by this world, Paul now affirms that a true Christian's 'citizenship is in heaven'. James Moffatt's famous version of this: 'you are a colony of heaven', though strictly not an accurate translation, brilliantly catches the flavour of what Paul is saying.

And this was apt language to employ in this letter because Philippi was a military colony of Rome. The city, we remind ourselves, had been refounded by the Emperor Octavian after military victory in 42 BC, renamed in honour of his daughter Philippi and repopulated with freedmen and veterans from the

Roman Army. Nowhere outside Italy was there any city more thoroughly Roman.

In Ben Witherington's words, 'The Philippians would have a very good idea what it meant to live by ruling principles that originated from afar.'[27] Its motto might well have been: 'When in Philippi do as the Romans do.' But the Christians in Philippi knew they owed allegiance to a different Emperor and another kingdom. Their rule of conduct was: 'When in Philippi do as Christ did'!

All expatriates try to keep alive the customs of their home country. Scotsmen abroad watch videos of the Highlands to the sound of bagpipes music! To an infinitely more significant degree, Christians are called, as Howard Marshall puts it, to 'follow the lifestyle of their native land'.[28]

Paul is reminding the church in Philippi that it was a colony of heaven set down in the midst of a colony of Rome, proud of its Roman citizenship. But when the apostles first preached the gospel in Philippi it exploded like a bomb dropped into the political status quo. 'These men,' went the complaint, 'are disturbing our peace ... subverting our Roman law and order' (Acts 16:20–21, *The Message*).

The new followers of Jesus became citizens of another kingdom, called to a wholly new politics of thinking and behaving. Sadly, this has often been misconstrued, by us as much as by our critics, as if we exist in a time-warp, intent only on preserving old values and permanently behind the times. But a colony of heaven is not backward looking, representing only 'the forces of conservatism'. On the contrary, we represent the future as citizens of the coming kingdom. Christians ought more often to be taken for revolutionaries than traditionalists!

In their bestselling book, *Resident Aliens*, Stanley Hauerwas and William Willimon put well the contrast Paul is drawing: '*Such behaviour is fine for everyone else, but not fine for you. You are special. You are different. You have a different story. You have a different set of values. You are a Christian.'*[29]

Uniquely, we live in two worlds but daily face the question put so typically by Martin Luther King: 'Will we march only to the music of time or will we, risking criticism and abuse, march to the soul-saving music of eternity?'

And notice the *outcome of such opposing ways of life.* One leads to destruction – it is a 'dead end' (v.19a). But notice what happens to the other!

We remind ourselves that the genuinely Christian mindset is not one which is 'set on earthly things'.

Enemies of the cross cannot be friends of the resurrection! But because our 'citizenship is in heaven' our hopes and horizons, destiny and dreams are bound up with heaven.

The implications of this are striking:

Firstly, we are characterised by *hope.* 'From heaven we await a Saviour, the Lord Jesus Christ.'

The Caesars and other significant benefactors in the ancient world were, at this very time, expropriating the title 'saviour' for their own self-glory. But as believers we are awaiting the arrival of the MIP (Most Important Person)!

Secondly, we must remember that salvation in the New Testament is predominantly *a future event* and experience. What a thought: that our life in Christ however wonderful now is but a tiny foretaste of what is yet to come!

Thirdly, our future hope is a decidedly *earthly hope.* Salvation is ultimately not about our going to heaven when we die; rather, heaven is coming here in the Person of the Saviour bent on reclaiming and renewing His entire creation.

That's why we'll need – and will assuredly receive – brand new, resurrection bodies. But to say that is to take a sneak look at the last page of the exciting final chapter in the different story we are enacting. And for that we have to wait with eager expectation.

3:21

This marvellous statement fittingly rounds off the argument which began in 2:1 and subtly mirrors 2:11.

At times in its history, the Church has sadly downplayed the value of the material creation and, in particular, of our physical bodies. But we do not become more spiritual by denigrating the physical which God saw as good and our Saviour saw fit to assume at Bethlehem.

Paul is not contrasting our 'lowly' body with something 'higher' or 'more spiritual'. He is contrasting our present 'body of humiliation' with our future 'body of glory'. For sin, disease and ageing do humiliate us. Early in my ministry, I stood by the hospital bed of a close friend whose body was shrivelled up by the cancer that killed him. I watched my own mother's dignity reduced by Alzheimer's. Yes, 'body of humiliation' well describes our current frailty.

Yet we remember that it was just this same physical, flesh and blood body that the Son of God honoured in His incarnation, and offered on the cross for our salvation. By doing so He affirmed God's intention to redeem us body and soul.

By His bodily resurrection from the dead, He majestically affirmed the goodness of God's original creation even as He magnificently inaugurated the new creation.

This is our sure and certain hope for all our friends and family who die 'in Christ'. Again the match with 2:5–11 assures us that the Father's glory which Jesus went through death to share, He will share with us, in turn, in resurrection.

Our first creation body may be ravaged by age and disease and succumb to death but our new creation body is guaranteed to be resplendent with glory. Praise the Lord!

Prayer and Reflection

Lord Jesus, knowing You has revolutionised my whole outlook.
You have given me a new life and a new ambition – to glorify
  You in all that I do.
You have given me a new focus and are helping me to do fewer
  things and to do them better!
It scares me that it is possible to become an enemy of Your cross.
Purify my life of all that would prevent me being a friend of
  Your cross.
Thank You once more, Lord, that I no longer need to live out
  of my past but can live out of Your future.
Thank You for the prize of the upward call of God in Christ
  Jesus that beckons us on.
Thank You for the sure and certain hope of resurrection that
  makes life, not death, the end of the story.
In Jesus' name,
Amen.

- 'You are different: you have a different story. You have a
  different set of values ...' How can we live sharply distinctive
  Christian lives without becoming a holier-than-thou ghetto?

- How should the 'politics of the kingdom of God' disturb the
  political and social conventions under which you live?

- Review how the story Paul tells in 3:4–21 mirrors the story
  told of Jesus in 2:5–11.

PHILIPPIANS

4:1-9 God's peace

¹Therefore, my brothers, you whom I love and long for, my joy and crown, that is how you should stand firm in the Lord, dear friends!

Exhortations
²I plead with Euodia and I plead with Syntyche to agree with each other in the Lord. ³Yes, and I ask you, loyal yokefellow, help these women who have contended at my side in the cause of the gospel, along with Clement and the rest of my fellow-workers, whose names are in the book of life.

⁴Rejoice in the Lord always. I will say it again: Rejoice! ⁵Let your gentleness be evident to all. The Lord is near. ⁶Do not be anxious about anything, but in everything, by prayer and petition, with thanksgiving, present your requests to God. ⁷And the peace of God, which transcends all understanding, will guard your hearts and your minds in Christ Jesus.

⁸Finally, brothers, whatever is true, whatever is noble, whatever is right, whatever is pure, whatever is lovely, whatever is admirable – if anything is excellent or praiseworthy – think about such things. ⁹Whatever you have learned or received or heard from me, or seen in me – put it into practice. And the God of peace will be with you.

As Paul moves to his closing exhortations, he expresses once again his deep affection for the Philippians. He addresses them very warmly as his loved and longed-for friends and family.

Interestingly, there were various set patterns for letters in the ancient world and Philippians has been identified by scholars as a classic *'letter of friendship'*. True friends and family, in Ben Witherington's words, 'love each other and look out for each other, including financially'. This is how it is between Paul and the Philippians.

Furthermore he calls them his 'joy and crown', expressions

which seem to look forward to the coming of Jesus. Paul, not wanting to have ministered in vain, hopes to meet Jesus then with joy because they are the fruit of his labours. He hopes to 'wear' the Philippians like a victor's wreath, confident that they will be the reason he will not appear empty-handed before the Lord. How remarkable that our lives are so bound up together as Christians.

It was for the joy set before Him of fulfilling the Father's will to save us that the Lord Jesus endured His shameful cross. It was with a view to being crowned with glory and honour as our Truly Human representative that Jesus tasted death for every one of us. Remembering this will nerve us – as it nerved the Philippians – to 'stand firm in the Lord' knowing we are loved, not just by His servants, but by the Master Himself.

4:2-3 Christians United!

Every Sunday is a celebration that God raised Jesus from the dead. By doing this God put His stamp of approval on the 'mindset' of Jesus which led Him not to look out for His own interests, but to humble Himself and become obedient unto death for us. Paul vividly pictured this 'mindset' in chapter 2 and commended it by his own testimony in chapter 3. It is this cruciform mindset that Paul now urges on two quarrelling women in the church at Philippi.

From what we know of the social background and the fact that Paul mentions their names, we may conclude that they were two important women leaders in the church.

Euodia and Syntyche had been Paul's co-workers along with Clement and an unnamed 'true companion' who, some scholars speculate, could have been Luke. So their disagreement is unlikely to have been some women's tiff but a serious disagreement about how the gospel should be practised in Philippi. Perhaps one of them was opting for a safety-first policy by favouring returning to the social shelter of overt Judaism or compromising with the Roman authorities. Paul implores them both courageously to embrace that mindset which was in Christ Jesus.

And, because Jesus died but rose again from the dead, His Book of Remembrance is turned into the Book of Life! Nobody stays dead whose name is written there by the One who lives 'in the power of an indestructible life'.

4:4 Rejoice again!

In this 'letter of joy' there can be no greater reason for rejoicing than knowing that we wake up each day in the same world as the Risen Jesus. He is alive and well. He is coming to reign. Why is Paul so insistent on the need to rejoice? Because joy is the hallmark of God's Easter people and to be otherwise minded is to rob the gospel of its attractiveness.

The story is told of the English vicar who, when asked by a colleague what he expected after death, replied: 'Well, if it comes to that, I suppose I shall enter into eternal bliss, but I really wish you wouldn't bring up such depressing subjects'!

But, as Peter Kreeft says well, 'Joy bubbles and brims at the heart of God, the heart of reality. God is an overflowing fountain of joy, a volcanic explosion of joy, a trillion burning suns of joy.'[30] It would break our hearts, if we touched a mere drop of this joy at its source. But we do touch a drop of God's joy in human love, catch a glimpse of it in the beauties of nature, or hear a remote echo of it in great music.

Above all, in knowing Jesus crucified and risen and coming again, we savour the taste of authentic joy in the flavourless tracks of everyday life. Even in the shadow of death, our hearts are strangely lifted by this joy as if of a distant but sure light at the end of the valley.

4:5a

Paul wants the Philippians to be known for their 'gentleness'. It is not easy to pin this word down in English translation.

Howard Marshall helpfully comments that 'the word suggests "magnanimity", the ability to remain reasonable and unperturbed when confronted by difficult people and to treat them calmly and fairly'.

Frank Thielman points to the use made of this word in the Jewish Book of Wisdom in a context where evil people who don't believe in the afterlife want to go out with a bang but meet opposition from a righteous man who disapproves of their irresponsible merriment. The evil men decide to persecute the righteous man to find out how 'gentle' he is and to 'make trial of his forbearance'. So, Thielman concludes, 'the term "gentleness" was often used of an attitude of kindness where the normal response was retaliation.'[31]

This is precisely the attitude of magnanimity and forbearance that Jesus displayed as He refused to revile His detractors and persecutors (2 Cor. 10:1; 1 Pet. 2:23).

What a wonderful change the gospel can bring about even in us to overcome our normal grumpiness. Whether tempted to lash out at those who are opposing us or to explode in exasperation with irritating people, the grace of God can produce in us Christ-like responses and reactions.

4:5b The Lord is near

How reassuring to be reminded that 'the Lord is near'. We could take this in two senses, just as the Philippians no doubt could have done.

On the one hand, 'The Lord is near' in that His second coming is looked for with eager expectation. Paul has constantly sought to lift the eyes of the Philippians to the horizon to live in the light of our Lord and Saviour's final arrival on the scene. At the same time 'to live is Christ' and here and now we can know the Lord's presence with us.

Maybe Paul deliberately lets the ambiguity stand. As Gordon Fee comments, this is the nearest Paul got to a holy double-entendre!

On the one hand, Paul is probably echoing the psalmist when, for example, he said that 'The LORD is near ... to all who call on him in truth' (Psa. 145:18). Scriptures like this would prompt the thought of prayer which Paul takes up in the very next breath (v.6).

On the other hand, throughout the letter, Paul has been strengthening the Philippians' morale with the conviction that the next important event that settles the course of human destiny is not the visit of any Roman Caesar but the appearance of the Lord of history Himself. We can live confidently in the nearness of the Lord whether that is temporal or spatial.

Either way, with them, we can rejoice, forbear and pray, because the Lord we love is closer and nearer to us than we think.

4:6 Pray with thanksgiving

To stop worrying is easier said than done! One doctor analysed his patients' fears as 40 per cent who worried over things that simply never happened, 30 per cent worried about past events now totally outside their control, 12 per cent were unduly anxious about their health though their only illness, he said, was a swollen imagination, 10 per cent were concerned for their families though in most cases their concerns were groundless. Only in 8 per cent of the cases did the worries have a basis in conditions which could be treated. I know – you're one of the 8 per cent!

And to you Paul might say, 'At least stop worrying long enough to pray!' Of course the Philippians' anxieties were more likely to have been caused by the social pressure of living differently as followers of Jesus, 'resident aliens' in an increasingly suspicious environment where allegiance was to Caesar and all things Roman.

But if we can work on the principle that the larger covers the lesser, then we can include here our more domestic but equally pressing anxieties – about the onset of old age, or paying the mortgage, or handling teenagers, or coping with stress in business, or concerns over health.

The same principle applies that we should not allow worries to stifle praise. Some prayer lists, Spurgeon said, are a recital of our unbelief. If we surround our needful burdens and petitions with as much thanksgiving as we can muster, then we will gain the courage to be quite specific with God about exactly what we want Him to do for us.

4:7 The guardian peace of God

The Philippians lived under an all-embracing political regime – the Imperial Roman Empire – which prided itself on having subjugated the known world so bringing to every nation the benefits of the '*pax Romana*', the Roman peace.

This Roman peace was maintained by garrisoning troops all around the Empire to put down uprisings and to quell dissent. In the final analysis Rome kept its peace by the crosses it erected to execute those who disturbed that peace.

Residents in the colony of heaven, however, are garrisoned in their hearts by heaven's peace. This heartfelt peace of God surpasses any merely natural way of understanding peace.

The peace of God is a mighty confidence when everything else is falling apart; this is the peace of Galilee in storm and Gethsemane in crisis. This peace, too, is established by the cross Rome erected on which Jesus died!

Thomas Merton once said, 'We are not at peace with others because we are not at peace with ourselves, and we are not at peace with ourselves because we are not at peace with God.' How true.

But to know Jesus as Lord is to know the peace that is forged in the crucible of Calvary.

As Ray Anderson observes, 'Serenity is not being in control but being under control.'[32]

So today, whatever is disturbing you, the Holy Spirit wants to speak to your troubled heart and fretful mind and say: 'Be at peace, be at peace, your Lord is near.'

4:8 Think the best

The list of virtues Paul now gives is not a particularly Christian one but could have been affirmed by many people in the ancient world.

What this implies is put well by Frank Thielman: 'This list with its admonition to look for the virtues in the wider world, reminds the Philippians that, although society sometimes seems hostile and evil, it is still part of God's world and contains much good that the believer can affirm.'

Understandably, this list has often been used as a motto by Christians on a moral campaign to clean up the media.

Now, of course, a poisonous mental diet will damage your spiritual health. But it would be sad if this text were read only in a proscriptive, negative way.

The Philippian church is called, as we are, to be an alternative assembly, representing the politics of heaven. As such the Church is inherently *counter-cultural*. That is, the Church is called to resist the forces of society that would twist its life out of God's shape and into conformity with the godlessness around it. But being *counter-cultural* is not the same as being *anti-cultural*! While we must resist the poison that drip-feeds into our souls every day from a rebellious world, we must equally relish every vestige of God's good creation that we can. Wherever and whenever we can we must echo God's original endorsement of His creativity and say, 'That is good, very good.'

Did the Philippians manage to do this with Roman roadbuilding and Greek art and architecture?

Looked at positively, Paul's exhortation is a glorious invitation to explore every part of God's creation with childlike curiosity. He encourages us to let our imagination take wing and range over all the God-given landscape of loveliness and excellence.

So, in the midst of your anxiety, take time out, prayerfully and thankfully, to feel the fur of a cat, trace a shaft of sunlight, enjoy the smell of rain on mown grass, find the wisdom in an old woman's face, relish the magic of choral music, gaze with wonder at great paintings. You may rediscover that in a thousand ways, in this fallen yet still beautiful world we can catch a glimpse of creation's original glory and even now taste the goodness conceived in the holy, healthy mind of the Maker.

4:9 The presence of the God of Peace

Paul was apostle, spiritual father, friend and mentor to the Philippians. He writes to them out of love for them and to promote their spiritual progress. He has just urged them to fill their minds with good things: now he wants to remind them to do, as well as think, good things.

What the Philippians have 'learned' is the full content of Christian instruction, the skills of how to walk and talk as disciples of Jesus. In referring to what they have 'received', Paul uses the standard word for tradition that is handed down, sometimes specific like the tradition of the Last Supper or, more generally, like the gospel handed down from the apostles to their successors. What they had 'heard and seen' refers to their firsthand knowledge of Paul's own teaching and the way he modelled a Christ-centred way of life when among them.

'Men and women return again and again to the few who have mastered the spiritual secret, whose life is hid with Christ in God.' So wrote Robert Murray M'Cheyne who, himself, well merits his place in that saintly category.

If the Philippians practise what they have heard preached by Paul and seen exemplified in him and others, then the God of peace will be with them. The God known in the gospel, the God and Father of Jesus is the God who paid the price of reconciliation, restores wholeness and promotes harmony and unity.

4:10–23 God's provision

[10]I rejoice greatly in the Lord that at last you have renewed your concern for me. Indeed, you have been concerned, but you had no opportunity to show it. [11]I am not saying this because I am in need, for I have learned to be content whatever the circumstances. [12]I know what it is to be in need, and I know what it is to have plenty. I have learned the secret of being content in any and every situation, whether well fed or hungry, whether living in plenty or in want. [13]I can do everything through him who gives me strength.

[14]Yet it was good of you to share in my troubles. [15]Moreover, as you Philippians know, in the early days of your acquaintance with the gospel, when I set out from Macedonia, not one church shared with me in the matter of giving and receiving, except you only; [16]for even when I was in Thessalonica, you sent me aid again and again when I was in need. [17]Not that I am looking for a gift, but I am looking for what may be credited to your account. [18]I have received full payment and even more; I am amply supplied, now that I have received from Epaphroditus the gifts you sent. They are a fragrant offering, an acceptable sacrifice, pleasing to God. [19]And my God will meet all your needs according to his glorious riches in Christ Jesus.

[20]To our God and Father be glory for ever and ever. Amen.

Final Greetings
[21]Greet all the saints in Christ Jesus. The brothers who are with me send greetings. [22]All the saints send you greetings, especially those who belong to Caesar's household.

[23]The grace of the Lord Jesus Christ be with your spirit. Amen.

4:10–11 Giving and receiving

'I have learned to be content.' What a striking testimony and one

we surely aspire to. It has to be admitted, of course, that the Christian Church has a tragic history of misusing this text to justify its complacency. Even worse, Paul's testimony has sometimes been used to suppress righteous protest, or quell justifiable discontent with injustice. We twist this text if we try to use it to cut the nerve of ambition or to put a stop to progress. That said, we are all experiencing nowadays a world of raging resentment and a clamour for rights, evidenced by a rising tide of litigation.

People are driven by unsatisfied and unsatisfiable expectations and are prey to rampant desires for pleasures which satiate but do not satisfy the soul, and too often lead to unhealthy addictions.

Who can teach us the 'secret of contentment'?

The Stoic philosophers tried by employing this very term Paul uses – 'self-sufficiency' – to emphasise the aloofness and detachment of the wise man, unruffled by emotions. I suspect the English adopted this philosophy as the creed of the stiff upper lip!

But no one can accuse Paul of being aloof, or emotionally cold yet he still claims to be content. Paul has learned the secret of sufficiency in another school, the school of Christ. The resources he finds are not self-generated but are drawn from the deep well of Jesus Himself.

This could only have been where Martin Rinkart found the resources to conduct the funerals of 4,000 plague victims and still write in 1637:

Now thank we all our God,
With hearts and hands and voices;
Who wondrous things hath done,
In whom His world rejoices;
Who from our mother's arms
Hath blessed us on our way
With countless gifts of love,
And still is ours today.

4:12 The secret of adequacy

Paul has learned contentment in both highs and lows, not least financial ones. He is writing out of pastoral concern for the Philippians whose most insistent pressure was economic.

In interpreting this text, there is clearly no room for some glib wealth and prosperity gospel. Paul has learned his contentment in good times and bad; he knows how to be abased and how to abound, how to handle financial difficulties and how to appreciate prosperity when it comes his way. This is a secret for all seasons, summer or winter.

This is a secret with many different applications.

Dr Paul Rees tells the story of H.G. Spafford, a friend of D.L. Moody, who lost his four daughters at sea when he sent them on ahead with their mother en route to Europe. On board another ship passing over the spot where his girls had drowned, Spafford found the grace to write the well-known gospel song: 'When peace like a river attendeth my way, when sorrows like sea billows roll; whatever my lot Thou hast taught me to say; it is well, it is well, with my soul.'

Clark Poling was a chaplain to the US Army in World War II who gave his lifebelt to drowning soldiers when their troopship, *The Dorchester*, was torpedoed. Before leaving on his last voyage, Poling had written home to his parents: 'I know I shall have your prayers; but please, don't pray simply that God will keep me safe. War is a dangerous business. Pray that God will make me adequate.' That's it exactly. And God did. And Paul would have applauded.

4:13 Ready for anything

We are looking at the secret of adequacy or contentment. Paul underlines his point with the gripping statement: 'I can do all things through Christ who strengthens me.'

Even as we enjoy the promise this contains, we need to heed a warning about taking texts out of context. Someone has said that this is the most abused text in the Bible. It is often quoted as a panacea for all ills, a sure-fire recipe for doing impossible miracles. No, the reality is more humdrum and infinitely more spiritual than that!

Read in the light of the previous verses '*all things*' in this context, can only mean all things encountered in the course of Paul's apostolic ministry. In other words, empowered by Jesus, Paul has been able to cope with whatever life has thrown at him in the pursuance of his God-given commission. J.B. Phillips caught the flavour of Paul's testimony perfectly when he translated: 'I am *ready for anything* through the strength of the one who lives within me' (my italics). Ready for anything exactly captures it!

Martin Luther King wrote to his imagined opponents: 'We shall match your capacity to inflict suffering by our capacity to endure suffering ... Do to us what you will and we shall continue to love you ... Send your hooded perpetrators of violence into our community at the midnight hour and beat us and leave us half dead and we shall still love you ...'[33]

Such is the indomitable resilience of those whom Christ empowers to be 'ready for anything'!

4:14–17 Money matters

Despite confidently assuring his friends that he is 'ready for anything' through the strength of Christ within him, Paul is concerned not to sound ungrateful for the gift the Philippians have sent him. 'You have done well to share in my trouble,' he hurriedly adds (v.14).

Despite having learned the secret of contentment in any and every situation, whether in need or in plenty, Paul does not want to give the impression that he is a lone-ranger, a self-sufficient independent spirit who has no need of anyone else. That would contradict what he teaches elsewhere about the inter-dependence of Christians in the Body of Christ. So he recalls gratefully the earlier support the Philippians had given him when he left Macedonia. You were the only church, he tells the Philippians, which shared with me in *giving and receiving*. Here is the heart of Paul's joy in his fellowship with the Philippians. Generous giving and humble receiving oil the wheels of love in the Church, and flow over into praise to God.

Paul is insistent that he neither needs (v.11) nor seeks (v.17) their support. He's not after their money. But he knows that such reciprocity builds up the Church in love and completes the joy of all.

4:18 Hot money!

Money is power and unleashes 'market forces'.

Is it possible to have money without being enslaved by the tyranny of money?

Is it possible to hold money without being corrupted by the love of money? But if money is power then it is not possible consistently to give money without giving oneself.

Paul presses the Philippians to believe that their material support for his own life is not, in itself, the point; it is, we might say, immaterial! What matters is the fruit it bears in their lives as they give and receive. This is the interest on the gift which Paul seeks.

'When we let go of money,' says Richard Foster, 'we are letting go of part of ourselves and part of our security. But this is precisely why it is important to do it. It makes life with God an adventure in the world, and that is worth living and giving for.'

Paul once more uses the language of Israel's worship – as in 2:17 where he describes his ministry as the *'leitourgia'* (or 'liturgy') of the faith. So here he considers their money gift a 'fragrant offering and sacrifice pleasing to God'.

'Hot money' is loot stolen from a bank which the police and underworld are both after. But fragrant money is that which no one has a tight fist around. In giving it with open hands and generous hearts, the Philippians show evidence of their fruitfulness in God's service. In receiving it with open heart, Paul recognises the gift as made to God as a sacrifice of praise. Such giving is a 'sweet smelling aroma'. It smells good to God because it has been offered back to Him on the sacrificial fire of the altar: now that *is* 'hot and holy money'!

4:19 God's supply-line

What a magnificent promise this is. 'This sentence is a master stroke,' says Gordon Fee.[34]

Eugene Peterson paraphrases it beautifully: 'You can be sure that God will take care of everything you need, his generosity exceeding even yours in the glory that pours from Jesus' (*The Message*).

Of course, the promise is not a blank cheque so that we might indulge our whims and desires but it is a cast-iron guarantee that God will meet all our legitimate needs.

And the measure of God's generosity in supplying our needs is 'his riches in glory in Christ Jesus'. God is gloriously rich in resources and can be trusted to fund His work and take care of His people. ' "Riches in glory," ' said Alexander Maclaren, 'seems to put them beyond our reach: but "in Christ Jesus" brings them down within our grasp.'

Christian giving and receiving is part of the joyful supply chain that maintains God's investment in our world. God gives most generously to those who give to others and to Him! No one is at a disadvantage by sacrificially supporting God's work. God is no one's debtor. He gives on a scale worthy of His wealth.

4:20–22 Grace in the end

The thought of God's gloriously lavish giving moves Paul to a characteristic burst of praise. 'To God be the glory, great things he has done!' 'Amen', 'Yes!' as if Paul is punching the air as winners do today.

His final greetings flow from this exultant praise. Every saint in Philippi is to be personally greeted on behalf of Paul and those of his colleagues who are with him at the time of writing. Intriguingly, Paul sends the greetings of the 'saints who are of

Caesar's household'.

This phrase refers to members of what we would call the 'civil service' or government administration – especially pertinent if the letter was written from Rome. Why does Paul mention them particularly as sending greetings to the Philippians? Had they perhaps in their travels visited Philippi and become acquainted with the church there? Or perhaps, as Howard Marshall suggests, there was a 'Philippi prayer-meeting' in Rome with a special burden to pray for the Philippian church?[35] Whatever the reason, Paul's greetings give another glimpse of the extraordinary interconnectedness of all who love Jesus.

There is a veritable 'network of grace' set up when Jesus changes our lives.

4:23

We sum up our discovery of Philippians by remembering that all Paul's letters are grace from start to finish. Philippians is no exception.

We might think of God's grace which opens the letter and bestows God's peace.

We might think of God's grace which begins a good work in our lives and is pledged to complete it at the day of Christ.

We relish the fact of being 'in it together', 'partakers of God's grace' together.

Think also of how God's providential grace can turn prisons into preaching centres, and enable His people to face death with extraordinary equanimity.

Above all, ponder again the amazing grace of our Lord Jesus Christ in not exploiting His advantages, in humbling Himself to be a servant and becoming obedient unto death.

And what grace it is that breaks a proud Pharisee and makes a Christ-obsessed apostle.

Recall the grace that makes us citizens of heaven's kingdom and raises our sights to a coming Saviour. Not to mention the transforming grace by which He changes our despised, death-ridden earthly bodies into radiant, resurrection bodies modelled on His.

It's all grace isn't it? Grace upon grace.

Gracious resilience that makes us ready for anything: gracious supply that means we lack for nothing!

Truly our life with Jesus is full of joy for it is grace from start to finish. Grace in the end is 'The grace of our Lord Jesus Christ be with you all. Yes!'

Prayer and Reflection

Lord, I realise only too well how I allow worry to corrode my
confidence in You.
I release to You the burden of anxiety I feel.
Lord, may Your Holy Spirit salt my prayers with reminders of
Your goodness, of memories of past mercies.
I confess Lord that too often I live in the past or out there, ahead
of myself in the uncertainty of 'what might be'.
Help me to live in Your presence in the 'eternal now'.
I long for 'a heart at leisure from itself' and I come to You now
for rest.
Make me ready for anything that comes my way in following
You.
I open myself to receive all that You want to give me, Lord,
So steady me and surprise me as You will.
According to Your unending grace,
Amen.

* How might Paul's words in this section have fitted the
  Philippians' situation as described in the introduction 'Seven
  things worth knowing about Philippians'?

* 'Security is not being in control but being under control.' How
  radical is this statement and how difficult to achieve? What
  difference would it make if it were true for you?

* What forces and factors in your life hinder your enjoyment
  of the gift of 'contentment' and how can we help each other
  to experience it?

* What has been the overall impact of meditating on Philippians
  again? Turn your conclusions into prayer and praise and
  decisions.

Resources

Reflections on Philippians:
The Message of Philippians by Alec Motyer in IVP's *The Bible Speaks Today* series is the best popular level exposition of the letter, written by a master-teacher.

The Life of Joy and *The Life of Peace* published in two volumes by Hodder & Stoughton contain the rich legacy of Martyn Lloyd-Jones. You can almost hear the 'Doctor's' voice in these typically perceptive and stirring expositions of the text of Philippians.

Commentaries on Philippians
Ben Witherington, III, *Friendship and Finances: The Letter of Paul to the Philippians* (Valley Forge: Trinity Press International, 1994), p.99.

Gordon Fee, *Paul's Letter to the Philippians* (Eerdmans: *The New International Commentary on the New Testament,* 1995). This is the classic commentary I would most recommend. As with everything Fee does, it combines massive scholarship with passionate concern and pastoral application.

Frank Thielman, *Philippians* (Zondervan: *The NIV Application Commentary,* 1995) – a good example of this increasing popular series, which accents contemporary application. But Thielman is a top-notch Pauline scholar and so the 'contemporary gravy' never obscures the 'biblical meat'.

Peter O'Brien, *Commentary on Philippians, New International Commentary* (Grand Rapids: Eerdmans, 1991).

On Acts
Acts by William Willimon in the Interpretation Series published by The John Knox Press, Atlanta: 1988 (UK, SCM Press) is a wonderful example of Willimon's flair and astute comment.

On Paul and his Gospel
The very best short, modern study of Paul, accessible to the general reader is Tom Wright's *What Saint Paul Really Said* (Oxford: Lion 1997). Superb stuff from Britain's leading New Testament scholar.

Advanced study
Ground-breaking-work on the analysis and theological message of the great passage on Christ (Philippians 2:5–11 – was done by Tom Wright and can be found in his academic essays on Paul *The Climax of the Covenant* (Edinburgh: T & T Clark: 1991) – the findings of which form the basis for a sermon on Tom's *New Tasks for a Renewed Church* (London: Hodder & Stoughton, 1991).

On Philippi
Peter Oakes, *Philippians, from People to Letter*, SNT (Cambridge: Cambridge University Press, 2001). Oakes' fascinating thesis on first-century life in Philippi helps to bring the church there to life.

Notes

1. Gordon Fee, *Paul's Letter to the Philippians, New International Commentary* (Grand Rapids: Eerdmans, 1995), p.11.

2. Ben Witherington, III, *Friendship and Finances: The Letter of Paul to the Philippians* (Valley Forge: Trinity Press International, 1994), p.99.

3. Richard Horsley in Richard Horsley (ed.), *Paul and Empire: Religion and Power in Roman Imperial Society* (Harrisburg: Trinity Press International, 1997), pp.206–214.
Εκκλησια seems a deliberate choice since other terms were available to Paul by which to describe religious gatherings, as Larry Hurtado points out in *The Origins of Christian Worship* (Carlisle: Paternoster Press, 1999), p.54.

4. Horsley, op. cit., p.141.

5. Horsley, op. cit., p.142.

6. Peter Oakes, *Philippians, from People to Letter*, SNT (Cambridge: Cambridge University Press, 2001), p.75.

7. Ibid., p.91

8. Ibid., p.100.

9. Gordon Fee, *Philippians*, op. cit., pp.2–23.

10. Ibid., p.47.

11. Ibid., p.53.

12. William H. Willimon, *Acts*, Interpretation Series (Atlanta: John Knox Press, 1988), p.136.

13. Ibid., p.140.

14. Alec Motyer, *The Richness of Christ, Studies in the Letter to the Philippians* (London: InterVarsity Fellowship, 1966), p.19.

15. N.T. Wright, 'Putting Paul Together Again' in ed. Jouette Basler, *Pauline Theology vol. 1* (Minneapolis: Fortress Press, 1994), p.207.

16. See N.T. Wright, *The Climax of the Covenant, Christ and the Law in Pauline Theology* (Edinburgh: T&T Clark, 1991), chapter 4. It was this seminal article that settled the meaning of '*harpagmon*' beyond reasonable doubt and spelled out its implications. For a popular exposition of the 'hymn' see Tom Wright, *New Tasks for a Renewed Church* (London: Hodder & Stoughton, 1991), pp.76–87.
See also my own use of the five circles device in my *A Passion for God's Story* (Carlisle: Paternoster, 2001), pp.26–30.

17. The quotations from Wright are – as far as I can recall – from his tape series on Philippians from Regent College, Vancouver audio library.

18. N.T. Wright, *The Climax of the Covenant*, op.cit., p.83.

19. P.T. Forsyth, *The Taste of Death and the Life of Grace* (London: James Clarke, 1901), p.32.

20. Gordon Fee, *Philippians*, op.cit., pp.220, 221.

21. Ibid., p.227.

22. Richard Hays, 'Crucified with Christ' in ed. Jouette Bassler, *Pauline Theology vol. 1* (Minneapolis: Fortress Press, 1994), p.241.

23. Søren Kierkegaard, *Purity of Heart is to Will One Thing* (London: Fontana, 1961), pp.191–192.

24. Os Guinness, *The Call* (Nashville: Thomas Nelson Publishers, 1998).

25. Douglas Webster, *A Passion for Christ: An Evangelical Christology* (Grand Rapids: Zondervan, 1987), p.21. I owe much to this brilliant and perceptive book.

26 Ibid., p.153.

27. Ben Witherington, *Friendship and Finances*, op. cit., p.99.

28. Howard Marshall, *The Epistle to the Philippians* (London: Epworth Press, 1991), p.103.

29. Stanley Hauerwas and William Willimon, *Resident Aliens* (Nashville: Abingdon Press, 1993), p.18.

30. Peter Kreeft, *Everything You Ever wanted to Know About*

Heaven, and never dreamed of asking (San Francisco: Ignatius Press, 1990), p.197.

31. Frank Thielman, *Philippians, NIV Application Commentary* (Grand Rapids: Zondervan, 1995), pp.218–219.

32. Ray S. Anderson, *Living the Spiritually Balanced Life* (Grand Rapids: Baker Books, 1998), p.143.

33. Martin Luther King, *Strength to Love* (London: Collins, 1963), pp.54–55.

34. Gordon Fee, *Philippians*, op.cit., p.452.

35. Howard Marshall, *Philippians*, op.cit., p.125.

National Distributors

UK: (and countries not listed below)
CWR, Waverley Abbey House, Waverley Lane, Farnham, Surrey GU9 8EP.
Tel: (01252) 784700 Outside UK (44) 1252 784700

AUSTRALIA: CMC Australasia, PO Box 519, Belmont, Victoria 3216.
Tel: (03) 5241 3288

CANADA: Cook Communications Ministries, PO Box 98, 55 Woodslee Avenue, Paris, Ontario.
Tel: 1800 263 2664

GHANA: Challenge Enterprises of Ghana, PO Box 5723, Accra.
Tel: (021) 222437/223249 Fax: (021) 226227

HONG KONG: Cross Communications Ltd, 1/F, 562A Nathan Road, Kowloon.
Tel: 2780 1188 Fax: 2770 6229

INDIA: Crystal Communications, 10-3-18/4/1, East Marredpally, Secunderabad – 500 026.
Tel/Fax: (040) 7732801

KENYA: Keswick Books and Gifts Ltd, PO Box 10242, Nairobi.
Tel: (02) 331692/226047 Fax: (02) 728557

MALAYSIA: Salvation Book Centre (M) Sdn Bhd, 23 Jalan SS 2/64, 47300 Petaling Jaya, Selangor.
Tel: (03) 78766411/78766797 Fax: (03) 78757066/78756360

NEW ZEALAND: CMC Australasia, PO Box 36015, Lower Hutt.
Tel: 0800 449 408 Fax: 0800 449 049

NIGERIA: FBFM, Helen Baugh House, 96 St Finbarr's College Road, Akoka, Lagos.
Tel: (01) 7747429/4700218/825775/827264

PHILIPPINES: OMF Literature Inc, 776 Boni Avenue, Mandaluyong City.
Tel: (02) 531 2183 Fax: (02) 531 1960

REPUBLIC OF IRELAND: Scripture Union, 40 Talbot Street, Dublin 1.
Tel: (01) 8363764

SINGAPORE: Armour Publishing Pte Ltd, Block 203A Henderson Road, 11–06 Henderson Industrial Park, Singapore 159546.
Tel: 6 276 9976 Fax: 6 276 7564

SOUTH AFRICA: Struik Christian Books, 80 MacKenzie Street, PO Box 1144, Cape Town 8000.
Tel: (021) 462 4360 Fax: (021) 461 3612

SRI LANKA: Christombu Books, 27 Hospital Street, Colombo 1.
Tel: (01) 433142/328909

TANZANIA: CLC Christian Book Centre, PO Box 1384, Mkwepu Street, Dar es Salaam.
Tel/Fax (022) 2119439

USA: Cook Communications Ministries, PO Box 98, 55 Woodslee Avenue, Paris, Ontario, Canada.
Tel: 1800 263 2664

ZIMBABWE: Word of Life Books, Shop 4, Memorial Building, 35 S Machel Avenue, Harare.
Tel: (04) 781305 Fax: (04) 774739

For email addresses, visit the CWR website: www.cwr.org.uk
CWR is a registered charity – number 294387

Trusted
All Over the World

Daily Devotionals

    Books and Videos

Day and Residential Courses

    Counselling Training

Biblical Study Courses

    Regional Seminars

Ministry to Women

CWR have been providing training and resources for Christians since the 1960s. From our headquarters at Waverley Abbey House we have been serving God's people with a vision to help apply God's Word to everyday life and relationships. The daily devotional *Every Day with Jesus* is read by over three-quarters of a million people in more than 150 countries, and our unique courses in biblical studies and pastoral care are respected all over the world.

For a free brochure about our seminars and courses or a catalogue of CWR resources please contact us at the following address:

**CWR,
Waverley Abbey House,
Waverley Lane,
Farnham,
Surrey GU9 8EP**

**Telephone: 01252 784700
Email: mail@cwr.org.uk
Website: www.cwr.org.uk**

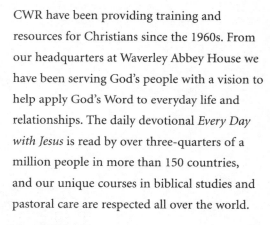

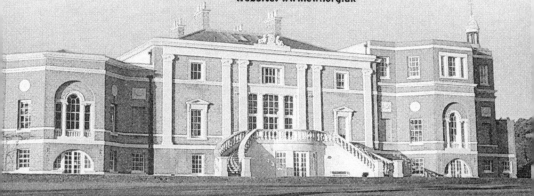

CWR   CRUSADE FOR WORLD REVIVAL   *Applying God's Word to everyday life and relationships*

Cover to Cover Bible Discovery: Psalms
Songs for all Seasons

Using the framework of the four seasons, *Songs for all Seasons* invites you to explore the world of the Psalms, the songbook of the Bible.

£7.99
ISBN: 1-85345-282-3

Cover to Cover
Through the Bible as it happened

Selwyn Hughes & Trevor J. Partridge

- Chronological one-year programme
- 365 undated readings – start any time of the year
- An overview of each Bible book with charts, maps, diagrams and illustrations.

Content previously published as *Through the Bible Every Day in One Year*

£9.95
ISBN: 1-85345-136-3

God's People
Through the Bible Character by Character

Selwyn Hughes & Trevor J. Partridge

- One-year programme with 58 Bible characters
- 365 undated readings – start any time of the year
- Selected readings taking approximately 10 to 15 minutes each day.

Content previously published as *Character by Character*

£9.95
ISBN: 1-85345-160-6

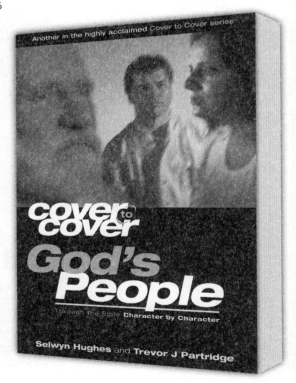

God's Story
Through the Bible Promise by Promise

Philip Greenslade

- Through the Bible promise by promise
- 365 undated readings – start any time of the year
- Daily readings reveal the relationship between the Old and New Testaments

£9.95

ISBN: 1-85345-186-X

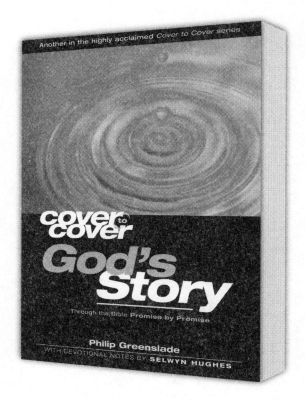